Bankruptcy Magic

THE LIFE-CHANGING POWER OF DEBT RELIEF WITH DIGNITY

Adrienne Hines

Foreword by DAVID PEPPER

Adrienne Hines-- 1st ed.
Chief Editor, Shannon Buritz
ISBN: 978-1-954757-53-0

For Zoe.

Every word in this book carries the echo of your belief in me.
Your fierce encouragement, boundless love, and unshakable
faith in my voice gave me the courage to step into my purpose.
You reminded me—again and again—that my work matters,
that people need to hear this, and that I was capable of more
than I ever dared to imagine. This book exists because of you.

It is also dedicated to everyone who has ever felt crushed
under the weight of debt and shame, believing they
were alone. You are not. There is a way forward, and
you deserve the chance to take it with dignity.

Zoe, I will spend the rest of my life honoring you.

Contents

Foreword

For too many American families, life these days can feel like a game of Monopoly.

One you are losing.

You know the feeling....that moment in the game when your opponents own most of the properties: Boardwalk, Park Place, and the other really expensive ones.

When your cash is down to a few bills.

When, everywhere on the board, you face houses and hotels that will take the rest of your money, which means every move—each roll of the dice—could be the move that wipes you out.

You dread when your turn comes around, just hoping to survive it. Your only hope is to get lucky and hit Free Parking, which may buy you two or three more turns before your luck finally runs out. Heck, in Monopoly, at least, you're better off landing in jail for three turns.

Today, with rising costs and big corporations dominating too much of American life, more and more people are facing this same dread. But the predicament is coming in the real-life form of ever-increasing personal debt.

If that old Monopoly game were to be renamed in 2025, it would simply be called "Debt."

But compared to the board game, the consequences in real life are far more dire, and the risks are far more stressful.

Debt is causing constant stress and pressure. Debt is piling so high that being wiped out feels one bad move away—one unfortunate roll of the dice from collapse. Pitfalls and risks are far more complex and well-hidden than in a Boardwalk or Park Place hotel.

It is *because* of this sobering and stressful reality many Americans face that I'm so excited about *Bankruptcy Magic*.

Because to avoid or overcome the obstacles before you, you don't need a lucky roll.

You're not faced with an inevitable disaster.

For most, there is a clearer path out—one far more in your control.

As this book promises, there is "a roadmap to reclaiming your life." There are clear, practical steps you can take—and pitfalls you can actively avoid to climb out of your financial dilemma.

And I know no one better than Adrienne Hines to shine a light on that path out.

Adrienne has spent her legal career helping Americans do just that, guiding thousands of clients out of debt and back into financial health and personal empowerment.

In recent years, Adrienne has mastered social media, sharing vital lessons in digestible snippets with even more Americans. Her words and videos usually go viral, not just because of her technical know-how and easy-to-understand explainers but also because of her passion for helping those who will most benefit from her wise advice.

In this book, she combines all that experience, passion, and skill to give folks a practical user manual and resource. But as she makes clear, it's not simply a legal guide about money, debt, and the bankruptcy process. It's a roadmap—perhaps YOUR roadmap—to a life journey—an empowering one.

As she promises: "You're about to discover that you have more options than you ever imagined and that everything you envision is well within your reach."

And, as you'll see as you complete this book, Adrienne delivers.

- *David Pepper*
Author, "Saving Democracy" and "Laboratories of Autocracy"
Fellow, The Kettering Foundation

Introduction

For many people drowning in unmanageable debt, a successful outcome isn't just about getting rid of the debt—it's about having a clear path forward. Imagine knowing exactly how and when you'll be free of that financial burden. Picture a future where you understand the steps you'll take to get there, and you can finally see yourself living a life that's full and vibrant, no longer weighed down by the stress and anxiety of debt.

What has been holding you back from achieving that debt-free future? The answer is often rooted in fear and misunderstanding. Many people are scared of the word "bankruptcy," but that's just one part of the puzzle. The real issue is a lack of understanding about debt and how the American economic system works.

You might be making choices that seem helpful but are actually digging you deeper into the hole. For example, borrowing more money when you're already in debt is like offering a drink to someone trying to quit alcohol— it just doesn't help. Yet, this is the route many people take, thinking it's the right solution. They believe that getting a consolidation loan or borrowing more is the way to manage their debt. But these strategies often backfire, preventing you from reaching the financial stability you crave.

This book aims to break down those barriers, helping you understand where you are, how you got there, and most importantly, how to get out. Let's clear up the confusion and start making choices that genuinely work in your favor.

What comes to mind when you hear the word "bankruptcy"? This word often invokes fear—a fear that everything is over, that your financial life has come to an end. This fear is deeply ingrained, leading people to believe that bankruptcy is the final nail in the coffin of their financial future.

But here's the truth: bankruptcy isn't the end; it's a new beginning. Instead of closing doors, bankruptcy can actually open them. It's a way to turn your financial life around, offering you a fresh start.

It's no surprise that many people are suspicious of bankruptcy. The common belief is that filing for bankruptcy will ruin your credit, making it impossible to function in the financial world afterward. There's a strong conviction that bankruptcy is something to be avoided at all costs because it will destroy your life.

I want to challenge that belief. While bankruptcy does impact your credit, it doesn't have to ruin your life. In fact, it can be the very thing that saves it. I plan to guide you through what bankruptcy truly means for your credit and your future, helping you see that it's not the catastrophe you might think it is. Instead, it could be the key to unlocking a more stable and secure financial life.

When it comes to navigating debt and considering bankruptcy, many people feel like they're up against an invisible enemy. This enemy is a combination of myths, pressures, and deeply ingrained misconceptions.

The first enemy is the myth that debt is a moral failure. Many believe that accumulating debt reflects a personal flaw, but the truth is that debt is morally neutral. It's neither good nor bad; it's simply a financial tool that, when mismanaged, can lead to trouble.

Then there's the pressure from friends and family, who may not understand the complexities of finance. They often suggest solutions that feel comfortable or familiar but may actually be dangerous and unhelpful.

Another major enemy is the fear of credit bureaus and credit rating agencies. People are terrified of what bankruptcy might do to their credit score, to the point where it stops them from even considering it as an option. This fear is compounded by a sense of embarrassment and the belief that their financial life will be permanently ruined. I've noticed that this concern over credit scores has intensified in today's post-COVID world. People are more aware and anxious about their credit than ever before, often feeling like they live and die by their credit score.

In the following pages, I will help you confront and overcome these enemies, empowering you to make informed decisions about your financial future without being held back by myths, pressure, or fear. We will tackle some of the most significant questions keeping you up at night, including...

- *"Does bankruptcy stay on my credit for ten years? Can I do anything about it?"*

- *"Will my house or car be taken away if I file bankruptcy?"*
- *"If not bankruptcy, what are my options?"*

When it comes to navigating the complex world of debt and bankruptcy, you want someone who's been there and seen it all. I've been a lawyer for nearly 30 years, and during that time, I've focused on bankruptcy law. My journey began in law school when I interned with a federal bankruptcy judge who became my mentor. He saw a need in our community and encouraged me to start practicing bankruptcy law. I was reluctant at first, but once I began, I fell in love with the work, and I've been dedicated to advocating for my clients ever since.

In my practice in Northwest Ohio, I've helped thousands of clients and worked in five different bankruptcy courts. My experience has made me well-respected in my field, so much so that even outlets like The New York Times seek my opinion. But my work doesn't stop in the courtroom. I've also taken my expertise to social media, where I've become an authoritative figure. I use that platform to remove the shame and embarrassment often associated with debt, helping people forgive themselves and find empowerment in their financial journey.

I'm passionate about navigating people safely out of debt, and I'm here to guide you through this process with the knowledge, experience, and compassion that comes from nearly three decades of dedicated service. You will learn how the American economy works and recognize that some types of debt—especially the predatory ones—can be wiped away through bankruptcy. These debts have been designed to manipulate and take advantage of you, but once you understand that, you can begin to take back control of your life.

Success is reaching the end of this journey without hating yourself because you have debt. It's realizing that you're a normal, regular person in America and that having debt is not a moral failure. There is a safe and healthy solution to your debt problems, even if it seems scary at first. You don't have to carry the burden of guilt or moral responsibility for your debt. This newfound empowerment allows you to make healthier financial decisions for yourself and your family.

Over the years, I've received countless comments and messages from people who found themselves in a desperate, fearful place, feeling like they had no options left when it came to their debt. They stumbled upon my social media pages in a moment of panic, unsure of what to do next. But something made them stop, listen, and engage with the content I share. They watched my videos, asked questions, and slowly began to realize that there was a door to a solution—one that wasn't even locked.

I've seen the transformation that happens when someone steps through that door, and I've been privileged to guide thousands of people through it, both in my legal practice and online. The messages I receive from people who say I've changed their lives because they didn't know they had options—that's what drives me. I wrote this book to reach even more people, to show you that you're not alone and that there is a way out. You're not a victim of your debt. You're not just passively allowing it to consume you. You have the power to take control of your financial future, to step forward, and to handle your debt in a way that leads to a successful, fulfilling life.

This isn't just a guide to managing debt—it's a roadmap to reclaiming your life. You're about to discover that you have more options than you ever imagined and that everything you envision is well within your reach. So keep reading, be vigilant, and believe you will overcome this. Your debt doesn't define you—what you do next does. Let's take that next step together.

- Adrienne Hines

PART ONE

Understanding Debt
And Its Impact

CHAPTER ONE

The Emotional Burden of Debt

S hame lives in darkness. When people struggle with debt, especially when they're unable to meet their obligations and worry about how to pay their bills, feelings of shame and embarrassment often take over. You need to talk about these emotions, acknowledge them, and then move past them because you can't think clearly when fear, shame, or embarrassment lead your decisions.

Discussing these emotions upfront, acknowledging their weight, and then putting them aside can allow us to focus on the reality of the situation. From there, we can map out a solution. This chapter will help you do just that—recognize the feelings you may be experiencing and guide you toward thinking with clarity so you can move forward.

When someone realizes they're in serious debt, panic, fear, and anxiety usually come crashing down. But more than anything, people feel two powerful emotions: embarrassment and pressure. These are the words I hear most often from my clients.

One of the biggest hurdles to solving debt is facing its reality head-on. When you're constantly robbing Peter to pay Paul, it feels like you're in a cycle that never ends. You take one step forward, then two steps back. The pressure and embarrassment grow, making it almost impossible to make intelligent choices.

A client shared with me how crippling this pressure felt. Every phone call filled her with dread in the two years before filing for bankruptcy. Every piece of mail stressed her to the point that she stopped opening it altogether. She couldn't bear to see what was inside because she had no solutions in sight.

She described her situation as climbing a steep mountain. She had pushed herself far beyond her limits, going higher and higher, only to find herself stuck. She couldn't climb any further but couldn't get down safely. She was frozen on the side of that mountain, paralyzed by panic, pressure, and anxiety, with no clear direction on what to do next.

This is what debt can feel like: being stuck, unable to move forward or back, and a flood of emotions can make it impossible to find a way out. But the truth is, there is always a way.

Why Debt Feels Like Losing Control

When debt becomes overwhelming, many people feel like they've completely lost control of their finances. It's a natural reaction when nothing seems to be working, and panic sets in. When they hit that breaking point, most people will try to fix things in ways they feel they understand, like borrowing more money or taking out a home equity line of credit. These options might feel proactive at the time, but they often backfire.

The feeling of control quickly fades when these "solutions" don't work, and people realize that their efforts aren't making a difference. This can lead to even deeper feelings of fear and helplessness. Because of stigmas and misinformation, many won't talk to family or friends. Worse, the myths surrounding bankruptcy make people think that it will ruin them even more, preventing them from seeking help sooner.

I had a client who perfectly illustrated this feeling of losing control. When she first called me, she was in a state of panic, overwhelmed and crying because every effort she had made to handle her debt was failing. She had taken out a second loan, maxed out credit cards, and was on the verge of losing her home. Others had told her that bankruptcy would destroy her life even more. But once we sat down together, within 30 minutes, we had a road map for her.

That 30 minutes changed everything. She went from feeling powerless and defeated to understanding her options. By filing for bankruptcy, she was able to direct the process, take ownership of the situation, and regain control over her life. She even wrote me a thank you letter saying, "I can't believe that 30 minutes changed my life."

When people realize that bankruptcy is a legal and safe option, one they can control, they start to feel empowered. It's not just about avoiding disaster; it's about moving forward and taking ownership of the process. The feeling of control returns when you have a plan, and that sense of empowerment is what leads to optimism and peace about the future.

That's why bankruptcy can be such a game-changer. It's like having a Sherpa guide who knows the path and helps you get back on track. Instead of guessing and stumbling, you have a clear, legal way forward, and that sense of control is something that my clients often say changes everything for them.

The Impact of Shame and Judgment from Family and Friends

Family and friends often play a large role in the decisions we make, especially when it comes to something as significant as debt. In most cases, they genuinely want what's best for us. However, there's a lot of misunderstanding about debt relief, particularly bankruptcy, and myths get passed down through generations. These misconceptions often lead family members to discourage seeking help, even when it might be the best option.

People are frequently told that bankruptcy will ruin their lives—that they'll never own a home again or that it will prevent them from moving forward. In an attempt to protect, loved ones might offer this advice, but it's based on outdated or incorrect information. Many people delay getting the help they need because they fear judgment or are misinformed.

I had a client whose family had owned a farm for generations. For years, she and her husband hesitated to seek help for their debt because her parents and grandparents told her that filing for bankruptcy would prevent her from inheriting the family farm in the future. Despite not expecting to inherit anything for years, this belief kept them from exploring their options.

It took them several years to finally speak with a bankruptcy attorney, only to discover that filing for bankruptcy was actually in their best interest. By addressing their financial situation early, they secured their ability to inherit the family property without worry. The advice their well-meaning family had given them had been entirely wrong.

Once this couple understood their options, not only did they file for bankruptcy, but so did the woman's brother, who the same misconceptions had also held back. The tragic loss of his wife compounded his situation, and like many others, he had been innocently misinformed by those he trusted. Once the truth came out, two families were able to take action to improve their financial futures.

While family and friends may have your best interests at heart, they may not have the correct information. It's essential to seek professional advice before making decisions that could affect your financial trajectory.

The Moral Weight of Debt

One of the complexities I often see is how faith and religion shape a person's views on debt. Many people's religious beliefs suggest that taking on debt is a moral responsibility, something they must fully repay no matter the circumstances. The idea of "paying what you owe" can be deeply ingrained in their faith. However, this perspective fails to acknowledge that our economic system has largely removed morality from how debt works.

In America, debt is morally neutral. Bankruptcy, in particular, is designed to address specific types of predatory debt—medical bills, payday loans, and high-interest credit cards. These kinds of debts often trap the most vulnerable among us, and there's nothing moral about being stuck in that system. In fact, it's dangerous to remain in debt when it's impossible to pay off, and it's even more damaging when people are made to feel like failures for considering bankruptcy as a solution.

I remember a client whose faith leader strongly discouraged them from filing for bankruptcy. This person had incurred debt from a failed business, and the faith-based leader told them that they would face eternal punishment if they didn't pay it all back. The client was terrified and conflicted. They had trusted their religious community for guidance, and now, they felt torn between their spiritual beliefs and the harsh reality of their financial situation.

After a lot of inner struggle, this client ultimately decided to file for bankruptcy. It was a difficult decision but the best financial move they could make. Interestingly, the process also led them to leave their church. This was an extreme but necessary decision for someone deeply rooted in their faith. They needed to find a place that aligned with their practical needs and financial reality.

Faith-based perceptions about debt often don't adapt to the rapidly changing economy. These views can keep people out of the financial game for far too long, convincing them that they are solely responsible for debts that, in many cases, aren't even their fault. For example, consider a woman who co-signed on a house, a truck, and other family expenses with her husband. If her husband succumbs to addiction, leaves the family, or faces imprisonment, is she morally responsible for paying off everything alone? At what point do we acknowledge that her circumstances have changed beyond her control?

Faith-based teachings rarely account for the complexities of modern life and the economic systems that leave people trapped in debt. General, unsecured, non-priority debt isn't a personal failing—it's a byproduct of an economy that often preys on those who are least able to defend themselves. I would love for faith-based communities to offer practical, supportive advice that aligns with the realities people face today.

The Emotional Transformation After Bankruptcy

The emotional transformation my clients undergo after filing for bankruptcy is nothing short of remarkable. Most people come to me anxious, skeptical, and utterly convinced that there's no way out of their financial mess. They'll say, "That's crazy; it'll never work," or "I don't believe you." However, the change will be incredible once they take that step and start the bankruptcy process.

One of my clients, who's become a good friend, was in that exact situation. She dragged her feet for nine months, scared and unsure, with her family not fully supporting the decision. I kept encouraging her, and eventually, she realized she had no other choice but to move forward. The moment she made the decision, I was there to guide her and her husband through the process. Once everything was finalized, her entire demeanor shifted. She went from being fearful and hesitant to confident and self-assured.

Now, she's not just in control of her finances—she's empowered. She understands her goals, has a vision for her future, and even educates her family about their own finances. Filing for bankruptcy didn't break her; it gave her the freedom to rebuild. She's even considering starting a business, something she never would have dreamed of just a year ago.

That's the kind of transformation I see in almost all of my clients. Once they have a defined path forward, the relief is palpable. The weight of debt is lifted, and they regain control over their lives. The mental and emotional burden that comes with overwhelming debt often leads to anxiety and even mental health struggles, but once clients pass through what I call the "vortex of understanding," things start to get easier.

Filing for bankruptcy is like being rescued when you're clinging to the side of a cliff, thinking there's no way out. But suddenly, a helicopter swoops in, and you're lifted to safety. That's how it feels when you realize there's a solution to your debt problems, and that solution is within your control.

In reality, bankruptcy can open doors to opportunities you never thought possible. Take Walt Disney, HJ Heinz, and Henry Ford— all of these giants filed for bankruptcy before going on to build their empires. Even Dave Ramsey, the financial guru who advocates for paying back all your debts, filed for Chapter 7. He eliminated his debt and built a fortune, teaching people how to avoid doing precisely what he did.

Bankruptcy isn't the end—it can be the beginning of something much bigger. The myths surrounding it, fueled by things like

Monopoly, keep people trapped in debt for years. I like to talk about "reversing the Monopoly effect." We all remember thinking that bankruptcy was the absolute worst thing that could happen to us as we moved our little pewter figurines around the board. But once you break free from these types of misconceptions, you realize that failure is often just the first step toward success.

Turning the Key

Many people hesitate to seek legal help because they're afraid of being judged by professionals. As a bankruptcy attorney, I'm acutely aware of this and work hard to create a safe, non-judgmental environment for my clients. People often have this image of lawyers as snobby, power-hungry individuals who don't care. A friend of mine, who was also a client, once told me that finding an attorney felt like finding a therapist. You don't just pick someone off Google—you need to feel comfortable and valued.

She felt at ease with me because I showed my authentic self. I spoke to her in a language she understood, explained things differently until she got it, and simplified the process. I assured her that no matter what, I had seen it all. That's a big part of making someone feel safe—letting them know that no question is too crazy or embarrassing.

When people reach out for help, they want to know that someone believes in them, values their unique situation, and will do everything possible to protect them. As a lawyer, my goal is to let my clients know that I genuinely believe in what I do. I know how powerful bankruptcy can be in changing the trajectory of someone's life, especially when their marriage or family is suffering due to money problems.

I've heard stories from colleagues emphasizing how terrifying it can be for someone to walk into a lawyer's office. A friend told me about a client who was so nervous about meeting a lawyer that they stood on the office porch, trying to gather the courage to walk in. This happened even though the consultation was free and confidential. People fear being treated poorly, spoken down to, or even laughed at.

That's why it's so important for professionals like myself to recognize how emotionally overwhelming it can be to pick up the phone and ask for help. If someone finds the courage to make the call, it's my responsibility to ensure that their time isn't wasted and that they leave with the information they need to make an informed decision.

The biggest hurdle for most people isn't the financial aspect of debt—it's the emotional burden that comes with it. I've seen time and time again that the fears people have about bankruptcy—what others will think, how it will affect their lives—are often unfounded. As one of my clients reflected after her bankruptcy was complete, she realized that no one judged her how she feared they would. None of her friends or family chastised her. In fact, many didn't even know. And now, she openly talks about her experience with pride, asking herself, "Why did I ever care what people think?" She realized that the judgment she had feared was nothing compared to the joy and relief of taking action.

I want you to know that there's a way out, and it's often much more straightforward than you think. The emotional weight—the shame, the fear, the judgment—is what holds you back. But once you gather the courage to take that first step, you find the door to relief was never locked. You just need to turn the key.

KEY TAKEAWAYS

➤ Debt brings overwhelming feelings of shame, fear, and pressure, but addressing those emotions is essential to finding a solution.

➤ People often feel they've lost control when dealing with debt, leading them to make unhelpful decisions like borrowing more money or ignoring the problem entirely.

➤ Misunderstanding and judgment from family or faith-based communities can prevent individuals from seeking the help they need, especially when it comes to bankruptcy.

➤ Bankruptcy is a powerful tool that can provide relief and empower people to regain control over their financial future, leading to personal transformation.

➤ The hardest part is taking that first step to seek help, but once it's done, the sense of relief and control can open doors to new opportunities and a fresh start.

CHAPTER TWO

The Types of Debt

Debt is not one-size-fits-all. Each type of debt comes with its own set of consequences, potential solutions, and level of urgency. Understanding these differences can help you make more informed decisions about your financial situation. For example, how you handle paying federal taxes vastly differs from how you'd approach a mortgage or a payday loan.

There's a common misconception that debt can be divided into "good" and "bad." It's not that straightforward. When people in the financial world talk about good debt, they're referring to debt that helps you build wealth or success—like a mortgage or a student loan. Bad debt, on the other hand, is debt that drags you down, like high-interest credit card debt. But no one sets out to take on what they believe is "bad" debt.

For instance, you might have used a credit card to start your business. It felt like good debt at that moment because it was helping you reach your goal. However, if you can't pay it off in full at the end of the month, that debt starts morphing into something more dangerous. It's not just about how the debt starts; it's about how it evolves over time.

Visualizing Debt as a Pyramid

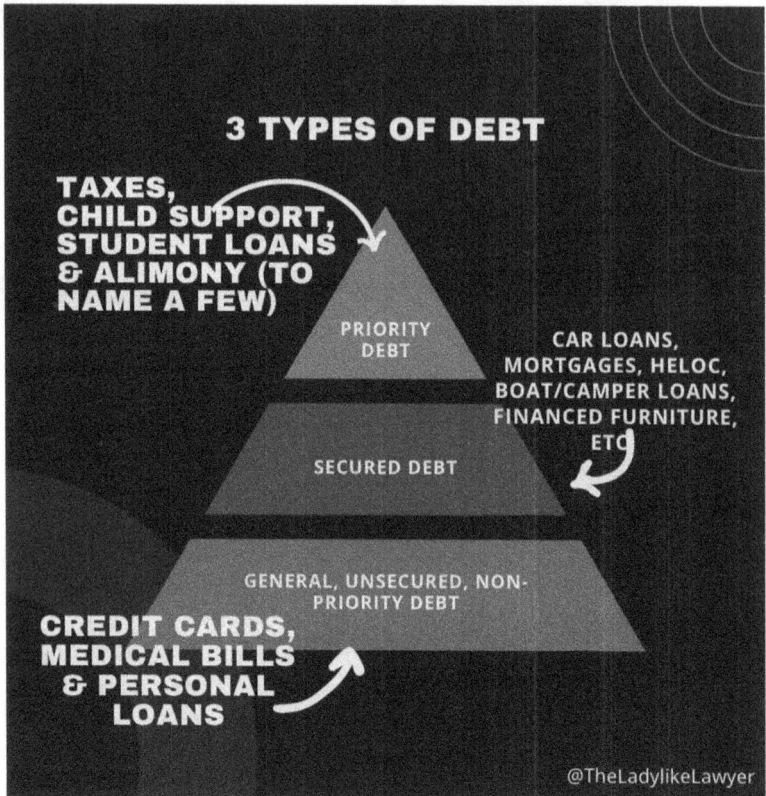

3 TYPES OF DEBT

TAXES, CHILD SUPPORT, STUDENT LOANS & ALIMONY (TO NAME A FEW)

PRIORITY DEBT

CAR LOANS, MORTGAGES, HELOC, BOAT/CAMPER LOANS, FINANCED FURNITURE, ETC

SECURED DEBT

GENERAL, UNSECURED, NON-PRIORITY DEBT

CREDIT CARDS, MEDICAL BILLS & PERSONAL LOANS

@TheLadylikeLawyer

I often use a pyramid to explain the hierarchy of debt. At the top of the pyramid is priority debt—those non-negotiables like taxes and child support. In the middle is secured debt, like your mortgage or car loan, which can be either good or bad depending on whether you're building positive or negative equity. At the bottom of the pyramid are the most dangerous types of debt: credit cards, medical bills, and payday loans. This base is the largest because it's where most people find themselves overwhelmed, and it's the kind of debt we need to eliminate first. Let's break down these three different types of debt:

1. **Priority Debt**

   Priority debts sit at the top of the debt pyramid because they simply won't go away. You can't hide from them; eventually, you'll have to address them. These include federal and state taxes, overpayments for Social Security or unemployment compensation, alimony, child support, and, for many, student loans. There are even specific cases, like if you committed a crime or caused damage, where those debts become priority because they're tied to legal obligations. In those instances, bankruptcy won't wipe them away.

   Knowing that these debts must be dealt with, it's easier to see where they should fit into your financial plan. For instance, it might be wise to borrow from your 401(k) to pay off federal taxes or catch up on child support because those are debts you can't get rid of in bankruptcy. On the other hand, it would be a mistake to use your retirement savings to pay off credit cards or payday loans. Those lower-level debts, which sit at the bottom of the pyramid, can be discharged in bankruptcy, and your 401(k) is protected.

2. **Secured Debt**

   Secured debts are loans that are backed by something you own—your home, your car, or even jewelry. If you don't make your payments, the lender has the right to take that item back. It can be good or bad, depending on the situation. If your mortgage is less than the value of your home, that's good debt because you're building equity. But if your car loan leaves you owing more than your car is worth, that's bad debt because you're stuck with negative equity. You must manage secure debt so that it works for you, not against you.

3. **Everything Else**

This is where the most dangerous debt lives: credit cards, payday loans, personal loans, and medical bills. Since the lender has nothing to repossess if you don't pay, they take on a higher risk. That's why they charge higher interest rates. This kind of debt can spiral out of control if you're not careful. High interest rates and predatory lending practices make it nearly impossible to get ahead. If you can't pay it off at the end of the month, this type of debt becomes a financial quicksand. The good news? This is the debt that can be addressed in bankruptcy if needed.

The Reality of Predatory Lending

Let me share a story about a couple who thought they were handling their debt responsibly, only to find themselves in a far worse situation. This husband and wife owned three cars, each worth less than $5,000—one was worth $3,500, another $4,500, and the third $5,000. Yet, each vehicle had a title loan lien on it for over $17,000. One loan was $17,000, another $18,000, and the last one over $20,000. They owed more than $55,000 on cars that were worth less than $15,000.

When they walked into the title loan company, they truly believed they were making a good decision. To them, taking out those loans seemed like a manageable solution to their financial problems. But it wasn't long before the weight of the debt became overwhelming. Once they realized what they were facing, they reached out to me, finally understanding that what they thought was "good debt" had never been good.

This story highlights a broader problem with predatory lending practices, particularly with title loans. Title loan companies take a security interest in your vehicle, often to scare you into paying them back. And while they might not always repossess low-value cars, they take advantage of people who don't fully understand the situation they're entering. My clients thought their vehicles were worth far more than they were. They believed they were securing a solid deal, but they were sinking deeper into bad debt.

This is unsecured financing at its worst, and I don't feel sorry for consumer lenders when my clients file for bankruptcy. These companies lend outrageous amounts at high interest to desperate people, knowing they'll likely never be able to repay the loan. It's a predatory system that pushes people further into financial hardship, and in cases like this, bankruptcy becomes the only viable solution.

Prioritizing Debt to Relieve Financial Stress

When clients fall on hard times, the first step is understanding what debts matter most. The key is to prioritize secured debts like your home mortgage or car loan over unsecured debts like credit cards. If you fall behind on your mortgage or car payments, the consequences come quickly—foreclosure or repossession—while missing a few credit card payments won't have the same immediate impact.

One of my clients came to me after realizing they had prioritized their credit cards, making minimum payments every month and letting their mortgage slip. Fortunately, they caught the problem before things got too far, but it was a wake-up call. What they should have done—and what I advise—is to ignore the credit card payments when money gets tight and focus on securing the essentials: your home, your car, your utilities, and food. Unsecured creditors can wait because they can't take anything from you immediately, and you have time to address those later.

As a bankruptcy lawyer, one of the first steps I take when working with clients is to help them organize and understand the types of debt they face. We start by cataloging everything—priority debts like taxes or child support, secured debts like homes or cars, and finally, non-priority, unsecured debts like credit cards, medical bills, and personal loans.

Once we've listed every type of debt, we can finally see the bigger picture. This is crucial because it allows us to understand the problem—and you can't have a solution until you know what the problem is. For many people, just getting all of their debt in front of them is the first step toward relief because it takes away the uncertainty and anxiety of not knowing what they're truly dealing with.

After breaking down the debts into their categories, we discuss the solutions for each pile. Non-priority, unsecured debt—like credit cards—is often the biggest source of financial stress. Remember that this type of debt can usually be managed through bankruptcy or other debt-relief options. Once my clients understand that there's a way to deal with credit card debt and medical bills without losing their homes or cars, their stress levels drop.

Turning Around Overwhelming Credit Card Debt

I've seen this situation with nearly every bankruptcy client I've worked with. People come to me overwhelmed, realizing that the path they're on—making minimum payments on their credit cards for the next 43 years—will keep them trapped in a cycle of debt. Even after all that time, they wouldn't be wealthier, just debt-free and poor. That's a terrifying reality to face, but it's also where we begin to make progress.

I had one client who was buried in credit card debt, making only the minimum payments each month. They felt stuck like there was no way out. However, once we began categorizing their debts, they started to understand that credit card debt is a non-priority debt. It's manipulative and predatory, designed to keep them trapped. When they realized that this type of debt could be addressed through a clear plan—whether it was bankruptcy or another solution—the emotional weight of embarrassment and shame started to lift.

Our goal was to eliminate their unsecured debt in five years or less. Once that plan was in place, it was like a dark box opened, and light poured in. The client could finally see a path forward, one where they weren't just drowning in debt but taking steps to get free of it.

The Long-Term Impact of Poor Debt Management

The consequences of managing debt poorly can be severe and long-lasting. If you don't address your debt problems within five years or less, you're squandering valuable time—time that could be spent building wealth, starting a business, or saving for retirement. The longer you carry unsecured debt, the more it drains your ability to invest in yourself and your future. Every month spent servicing high-interest debt is when you're not putting money toward something that will improve your financial situation.

In America, managing debt early is especially critical because your earning potential decreases once you retire. If you've spent your working years chipping away at unsecured debt without making significant progress, you'll find yourself in a precarious position later in life. Imagine reaching 62 with nothing left in your 401(k) because you've been pulling from it to stay afloat, only to still be in debt. This is a scenario I see far too often, and it's one of my biggest fears for clients.

Practical Steps for Sorting Through Good and Bad Debt

If you're struggling with both good and bad debt, you first need to sit down and pull your credit report. You can get a free one online, and while it may seem complicated at first, it's a critical tool for getting a clear picture of your financial situation. If you're working with a bankruptcy lawyer, we buy easy-to-read credit reports for clients, but you can do this independently.

Step 1: Make a Full Inventory of What You Owe and What You Own

Start by writing down every single person or company you owe money to, how much you owe, and what your minimum payments are. Equally important is knowing the value of your assets. How much do you owe on your car, and how much is it worth? Do the same for your house. You'd be surprised how many people don't know these figures, and once you do, you can tell if you're sitting on positive equity or drowning in negative equity.

If you don't know what your stuff is worth, it's impossible to figure out whether you're financially stable or in trouble. You need to know the value of your home, your car, and any other significant assets. Then, list all your unsecured debt—credit cards, medical bills, personal loans, even old debts like an apartment complex that charged you for damages years ago.

Step 2: Understand Your Equity

Once you've cataloged everything, assess whether you have positive or negative equity. Do you owe more on your car than it's worth? Is your home underwater, or do you have equity? This step is crucial in determining how to approach your debts.

Step 3: Face the Emotional Challenge

I understand that making this list is emotionally exhausting for most people. Confronting the reality of your financial situation is not easy, but it's necessary to take control. Once you have a complete picture, you can start making informed decisions about which debts to prioritize and what steps to take next to achieve financial freedom.

KEY TAKEAWAYS

➤ Debt comes in various forms, and understanding the differences between priority, secured, and unsecured debts is essential for managing your financial situation effectively.

➤ "Good" debt, like mortgages or student loans, can help build wealth, while "bad" debt, such as high-interest credit cards or payday loans, can quickly spiral out of control if not addressed.

➤ Prioritizing debt by focusing on secured obligations, like your home or car, before addressing unsecured debts is crucial to avoid severe financial consequences like foreclosure or repossession.

➤ Predatory lending practices, especially with unsecured financing, can trap borrowers in dangerous financial situations, but bankruptcy or debt relief can provide a way out.

➤ Taking the time to categorize and understand your debts is the first step toward relieving financial stress and building a plan for long-term financial success.

CHAPTER THREE

A Historical Perspective on Debt in America

L ike many topics we discuss in life, historical context is important because it helps you understand how we got here in the first place. When you see the bigger picture, you begin to realize that the debt you're struggling with isn't just a personal failure or something you're incapable of figuring out. You're part of a much larger system—a manipulative, predatory puzzle designed over time to take advantage of people.

When you recognize that, you can start letting go of the self-blame, shame, and guilt that often come with debt. It's not about being a bad person or being "bad" with money or making bad decisions. This system has been set up to confuse and manipulate you on purpose.

That kind of knowledge gives you power. It gives you the strength to stand up and make the necessary choices to help yourself and your family move forward. Understanding the history of debt allows you to start looking at your choices more realistically and with less judgment. When you do that, you can begin to fight for yourself in a way you may not have before.

How America's Economic History Shaped Our Culture of Spending and Borrowing

America's culture of spending and borrowing has deep roots in our economic history, particularly in the post-World War II era. After the war, a shift fundamentally changed how Americans viewed consumption. Soldiers returning home had been exposed to new products during their time overseas, like Coca-Cola, chocolate, and other conveniences they hadn't had before. Companies saw an opportunity and worked hard to make sure that, when those soldiers returned, they would want to continue enjoying those products.

This was the birth of modern consumerism in America. After the war, Americans had more disposable income than ever before, and companies were innovating at a rapid pace. Things like newfangled stoves, cars, and suburban homes became accessible to more people, and Americans found themselves with extra time and money to spend on products they didn't even know they needed.

Television played a huge role in fueling this culture of consumption. Not only did people watch TV for entertainment, but the advertising that came with it convinced them they needed these new products. Sponsors paid for shows, and those sponsors had to sell things to the viewers. It created a cycle where people were constantly being told they needed the latest and greatest product to make their lives better or easier.

This new consumer-driven mindset led to the rise of credit cards. The Diners Club card was the first credit card introduced, and others like Bank of America and American Express soon followed. Credit cards became a way for Americans to buy now and pay later, further embedding the idea that consumption was not only a way of life but an expectation.

With more money in their pockets and more products to buy, Americans fell deeper into consumerism. Companies like Hershey's and Frito-Lay worked hard to lobby Congress, ensuring that the consumer-driven world we live in today became the norm. They created a culture where convenience and consumption were king.

However, with the rise of consumerism came the rise of consumer debt. By the 1970s, Supreme Court rulings began loosening lending laws, allowing credit card companies and banks to take advantage of consumers. What started as a society rooted in thrift and moderation turned into one that constantly needed more. This shift opened the door for lenders to capitalize on our desire for convenience and comfort, leading to our credit-driven society today. What was once a nation that capped interest rates at 6% has become manipulative and predatory while consumer protections are continually being stripped away, leaving many Americans trapped in a cycle of debt.

The Evolution of Usury Laws in America

Usury laws have played a significant role in shaping lending practices in America. These laws cap the interest rates lenders can charge consumers, and this concept goes back to Biblical times. Even before the United States was officially formed, early American colonists set a cap on interest rates at 8%. After the Revolutionary War, when the states came together as a nation, they further reduced this cap to 6%. That was a strong start for protecting consumers.

But from then on, there has been a steady shift away from protecting people from high interest rates, especially after World War II. The safeguards that usury laws provided began to erode, with significant changes occurring in the 1970s. The Supreme Court case of *Marquette National Bank v. Omaha Service Corp., 439 U.S. 299* in 1978 was a key turning point. Before this case, each state had its own cap on interest rates, which applied to businesses operating within their state's border. But the ruling changed everything.

The court ruled that businesses could use the interest rate cap of the state where they were headquartered, regardless of where they conducted business. This opened the door for companies to move to states with little or no interest rate caps, and North Dakota was the first to eliminate its caps. Banks rushed to incorporate in North Dakota, allowing them to charge high interest rates in other states. As a result, most states had to raise or eliminate their caps to stay competitive.

Today, states still impose limits on Annual Percentage Rates (APR) for consumer loans, but the protections vary widely. Some states, like Arkansas, Maine, and Vermont, maintain strict APR limits as low as 17% to 18%, while others, like Georgia, allow rates as high as 60%. Some states, like Delaware, Ohio, and North Dakota, have no interest rate limits at all. This patchwork of regulations continues to influence how lenders operate, often at the expense of consumers.

The changes in usury laws have profoundly impacted specific communities, particularly those already at a financial disadvantage.

When credit becomes difficult to access, it affects people's ability to achieve what we often consider the "American Dream"—homeownership, education, and upward mobility. An example is the GI Bill, which, after World War II, provided a huge opportunity for many service members to purchase homes and move into the suburbs. However, this opportunity was not equally available to people of color or immigrants, which laid the groundwork for the vast income disparity we see in America today.

Communities that benefited from the GI Bill flourished, often becoming more affluent and less diverse over time. Meanwhile, communities of color and other marginalized groups were left behind. These groups—immigrants, minorities, single women, and others—were already starting from a place of financial disadvantage. When access to quality lending was further restricted, it created a cycle of poverty that has been incredibly difficult to break.

When living paycheck to paycheck, rising interest rates and limited lending options force you into difficult decisions. Someone with more financial resources might simply cut back on luxuries like dining out. But the trade-offs are much more dire for someone struggling to get by—you may have to choose between paying the mortgage or covering your credit card bills. This fragile financial state pushes people into the arms of predatory lenders, such as payday loan companies, which often set up shop in vulnerable communities. The lack of accessible, truthful information keeps them in a loop of making the same financial mistakes over and over again. This history shows that the system is designed to confuse and manipulate, not to protect. And knowing this can help you approach your financial decisions with less guilt and more clarity.

The Relationship Between Capitalism, Risk, and Debt in America

I discuss this powerful topic on my social media because it's crucial for people to understand the bigger picture. America is built on risk-taking. Our very foundation is rooted in people who made a tremendous effort to get here—and people who were brought here against their will. Early Colonial Americans were fleeing religious persecution, debtor's prisons, and oppressive systems. They took unimaginable risks to forge a new life. At the same time, enslaved people were violently forced into that same system—made to labor, build, and fuel an economy based on risks they never chose. That tension is part of our DNA: the pursuit of freedom, shadowed by the reality of stolen freedom.

In the early days of America, settlers climbed into covered wagons and headed into the unknown. They risked their lives for a shot at land, ownership, and independence—often on land that had already belonged to others. Families were lost, and yet others still made the journey. That's part of who we are: a nation shaped by risk, ambition, and belief in the promise of reward. But it's also a nation built on debt, extraction, and the bodies of people who had no choice at all. Capitalism in America was never just about freedom—it was also about control. To fully understand our relationship with risk and debt today, we have to be honest about that legacy.

You can't have a capitalist economy without encouraging risk. And that's why bankruptcy exists in America. It allows people to take those big risks without being completely destroyed if they fail. If you try to start a business and it doesn't work out, bankruptcy is there to give you a way to wipe the slate clean, dust yourself off, and try again. It's embedded in our belief system that success comes through failure. Walt Disney filed for bankruptcy. H.J. Heinz, the creator of the ketchup empire, filed for bankruptcy. These icons wouldn't exist if we didn't have a system that allows for failure and second chances.

Every new business, every new venture, involves someone facing fear—maybe even throwing up a little or sweating through their shirt—but we go for it anyway. The desire to try outweighs the fear of failure. That's where success comes from—the willingness to try. If we removed the safety net of bankruptcy, we would stifle that desire, making us all too cautious to take risks.

I had a client once who perfectly embodies the American spirit of risk-taking and innovation. He was an inventor, and let me tell you, this guy had a fire in him. He had come up with a revolutionary prototype for a scientific device that he was convinced would change the world. His enthusiasm was contagious—I even considered investing in him myself at one point because I believed in his vision. But, as many inventors and entrepreneurs do, he sank all of his money—and I mean *all* of it—into this invention. Unfortunately, the prototype wasn't fully functional yet, and he found himself in a situation that so many dreamers encounter: financial ruin.

He had drained their savings and was driving his wife crazy with his persistence, but he truly believed that this invention would work someday. And honestly, I think he will eventually succeed, just like so many other famous inventors who fell on their faces countless times before they made it big. Think about the story of disposable razor blades—they took decades to develop, and the inventor went into poverty more than once trying to make them work. But, ultimately, he succeeded, and it changed the world.

In America, we celebrate risk because we know that success often comes after failure. Most people don't realize how often they fail before getting it right. And that's what we miss when we only look at the outcome. Everyone with a little bit of hope and a willingness to take risks convinces themselves that their venture is worth it, and they push forward.

My inventor client is a perfect example of this. Despite their financial struggles, we were able to file for bankruptcy and give them a fresh start. I hope his invention will someday revolutionize the industry, and he'll be a billionaire. But even if it doesn't, he represents the very core of what America is about—taking risks, facing failure, and trying again. Not every business or invention will succeed, but for every idea that flops, there's a chance that the next idea will be the one that changes everything.

Generational Financial Behaviors: Breaking the Cycle

Financial behaviors often run deep through generations, and many people unknowingly inherit risky financial habits from their families. It's common to see the same mistakes being passed down from parent to child, even though these practices might be based on misunderstandings or outdated beliefs about money. When you grow up in poverty or in an environment where money is always tight, you often adopt creative strategies to make ends meet. But sometimes, these strategies are based on myths or misinformation about how finances really work.

I'll never forget a client who came to me before COVID. She and her family were struggling with their mortgage, and something stood out when I asked her to identify where they were behind—whether it was on their real estate, cars, or credit cards. They were behind on their mortgage but current on their credit cards. Naturally, I assumed they no longer wanted to keep their home, but that wasn't the case at all.

It turned out that this client had grown up with the belief, passed down through her family, that if you didn't pay your credit cards, the credit card company could garnish your wages faster than a mortgage company could foreclose on your home. So, in a moment of financial stress, they were prioritizing credit card payments over their mortgage. This belief was utterly backward, but it was a truth they held because they remembered their mother being garnished but never losing the house, so they thought that paying credit cards was the safest bet.

What they didn't realize was that times have changed. Back then, you could walk into your local bank and explain your mortgage troubles, and there was a good chance you'd get help. That's not how things work anymore, and continuing to operate with that outdated mindset led them down a path toward foreclosure. We were able to step in with a Chapter 13 bankruptcy to reorganize their debt and help them save their home, but this was a clear example of how deeply ingrained financial misunderstandings can impact generations. Breaking that cycle requires being open to new information and recognizing that some of the beliefs you've held onto might no longer apply. It's never too late to get the right advice and make better financial choices for yourself and your family.

Moving Forward with Knowledge and Confidence

Many people believe their personal choices are solely responsible for their debt, but a significant part of the problem stems from the deregulated consumer lending industry. When you see that the system is predatory by nature, you can start approaching your financial decisions with more care. It's not about blaming yourself for falling into a trap but recognizing that the system was built to make it easy to do so. When dealing with lenders, you're not just borrowing from a friendly institution but navigating a system designed to profit from your missteps. In essence, if you're "dancing with a cobra," it's crucial to recognize the danger for what it is rather than mistaking it for something harmless like a garter snake.

America is built on hopes and dreams. It's a country where we believe that anything is possible, where the next great invention or business could turn an ordinary person into a millionaire. This belief in the American Dream drives many of us to take risks, start businesses, or invest in what we believe could be the "next big thing." But this same spirit of hope and optimism can sometimes make us vulnerable to scams, especially when they promise quick wealth or an easy path to success.

It's not uncommon for people who have been scammed to feel a sense of shame or embarrassment, but in reality, they are acting on the very beliefs that America instills in all of us: that with enough risk and effort, anything is possible. That's why people continue to believe in their dreams, even when those dreams come with significant financial risks. Success doesn't come without failure, and failure is not the end of your story. By understanding the system clearly, recognizing the traps, and letting go of the shame associated with debt, you can move forward and take control of your financial future.

KEY TAKEAWAYS

➢ Understanding the history of debt reveals that the system is designed to manipulate and confuse consumers, allowing you to release the shame and self-blame often associated with debt.

➢ America's post-war culture of consumerism, fueled by credit cards and advertising, transformed thriftiness into a cycle of consumption and debt, creating a credit-driven society.

➢ Changes in usury laws, especially after the 1970s, opened the door for predatory lending practices that disproportionately impact marginalized communities, perpetuating financial disadvantage.

➢ The American spirit of risk-taking, embedded in our capitalist system, encourages entrepreneurship but often leads to financial pitfalls; bankruptcy offers a safety net for second chances.

➢ Generational financial behaviors can perpetuate risky habits and misunderstandings; breaking the cycle requires questioning outdated beliefs and seeking accurate, up-to-date financial advice.

PART TWO

Managing Debt and Finding Solutions

CHAPTER FOUR

How Debt Accumulates

When you take the time to dig deep into the root causes of debt, you achieve two powerful outcomes. First, you chip away at the stigma surrounding debt. That heavy cloud of shame that hovers over anyone facing financial challenges starts to lift when we collectively step back and see the bigger picture. Second, this awareness sets the stage for change so that you're equipped with the knowledge and tools to take meaningful steps toward a healthier financial future on the other side of the bankruptcy process.

I often say that debt happens *to* us, not because of us. While society might paint debt as a consequence of poor choices, the truth is far more complex. There are a handful of primary reasons people find themselves in a financial crisis and some of the most notable are: the death of a family member, job loss, major medical events (either to themselves or loved ones), divorce, scams and financial abuse, failed business ventures, and yes, even overspending. Let's break this down a bit more because, as you'll see, many of these are outside our control.

The Financial Fallout of Losing a Spouse

The death of a spouse can be financially devastating in ways that most people don't fully anticipate. Life insurance policies often have either lapsed or never existed, and savings may be minimal. Even more challenging is when the spouse left behind is financially unsophisticated—someone who has never handled the household finances. I've seen this firsthand in the year I found myself filing bankruptcy for five different widows of doctors.

What stood out about these cases was that every single widow had little to no experience managing money. These women had depended on their spouses, who, despite their medical expertise, had not planned for a future without them. These doctors didn't prioritize savings or retirement funds, assuming they would work and generate income for life. But when the unexpected happened, their widows were left with few resources and a social security check that was far smaller than anticipated.

Beyond the financial knowledge gap, there's the sheer emotional burden. Losing a spouse means stepping away from work—at least temporarily—to handle the practical and emotional demands of dealing with death. This time away impacts earnings, and the grief itself can make it difficult to focus and perform at work, further straining income.

Divorce

Divorce is another major life event that contributes to financial distress. When a marriage dissolves, assets are divided, but so are debts.

In addition to splitting what you own, you're also splitting what you owe, and legal fees can add up quickly. If one partner earns significantly more than the other, the lower-earning partner may find themselves unable to maintain their standard of living post-divorce. Additionally, child support and alimony payments can strain the paying partner financially, making it difficult to stay afloat.

Both situations—losing a spouse or going through a divorce—reveal an essential truth: when major life changes hit, they affect every aspect of your finances. Frequent conversations about life insurance, savings, and understanding basic household finances can make moving forward in either of these circumstances more manageable.

The Impact of Job Loss on Debt

Job loss, especially when unexpected, immediately halts your ability to cover your monthly expenses. Even if you've been diligent about living below your means and building a cushion of savings, the safety net doesn't always hold up as long as people hope it will.

Take, for example, the wave of layoffs that often follows when a manufacturing company decides to relocate operations overseas. The local workforce is left scrambling, and while some may have anticipated the shift, for most, the realization comes too late to meaningfully prepare. What happens next is a rapid decline in financial stability.

Most people believe they have enough savings to carry them through a rough period, but they don't anticipate how quickly that money can disappear. Even a substantial emergency fund—say $25,000—can vanish faster than expected when no income stream replenishes it. Many people use their savings as a buffer to stay current on debt, believing they'll find another job soon or that things will improve before the funds run dry. But when the job search stretches from weeks to months, those savings are whittled down, leaving little to nothing to fall back on.

Using savings to pay down debt isn't inherently wrong, but it becomes risky when it leaves you without a buffer for emergencies. If you're already in this position, know that seeking help, even if that means considering bankruptcy, is not a failure—it's a responsible step toward regaining control.

The High Cost of Medical Events

Medical events are among the most common—and devastating—reasons why people find themselves drowning in debt. One story that stands out vividly in my mind is that of an older couple who came to me for help. This couple, both in their early 60s, had been living a modest, comfortable life. The husband was 59 or 60 and intended to work for another five to ten years. But life had other plans. One day, he suffered a heart attack, which set off a chain of medical treatments and interventions—emergency life flight, heart surgery, cardiac therapy, and countless follow-up visits. Unfortunately, his job didn't offer great insurance coverage, so the bills quickly piled up.

Unable to return to work, they faced a reality many don't realize until it's too late: applying for Social Security disability can take up to two years, and even after approval, Medicare isn't available for another two years. Imagine being stuck in that limbo—no job income, no disability benefits, and no insurance. During this time, this couple accumulated over $60,000 in medical debt, spread across multiple providers.

What struck me most was their sense of responsibility and duty. They believed it was their obligation to pay their bills, especially to the hospital that saved his life. Month after month, they sacrificed essentials just to make payments they could barely afford. The wife was often in tears, and the husband was defiant whenever we spoke. They were not eating well, could not buy enough groceries, and had to skimp on the medications they needed. They even fell behind on property taxes—all in an attempt to manage this insurmountable debt.

Despite their best intentions and payments, the hospital sued them for the outstanding balance. This was the final straw that brought them to my office. I showed them that filing for bankruptcy wasn't a failure but a lifeline. It was a way to get out from under a burden they could never hope to pay off. And once we filed, they experienced a newfound peace. The weight of that $60,000 debt was lifted, and they could finally focus on their health and well-being without the constant stress of financial ruin.

A common belief that prevents people from seeking this type of help is that medical bills can't be included in bankruptcy. Another is that there's a special type of bankruptcy just for medical bills. Neither of these is true. Medical bills *can* be discharged in bankruptcy, just like credit card debt and other unsecured debts.

The impact of a serious medical event doesn't stop at the bills alone. It ripples through every aspect of a family's life. For example, when a child is diagnosed with a serious illness like leukemia, it's often the mother who steps away from her job to provide care. This means losing an income and facing added expenses—travel, hotels, time off work—all of which add up. The same happens when adult children care for elderly parents, known as the "sandwich generation." They find themselves stretched thin, both financially and emotionally, as they juggle caregiving and their own financial responsibilities.

The truth is, when someone in the family is ill, the whole family bears the cost. It's a strain that affects health, relationships, and mental well-being. Understanding this helps dismantle the myth that debt is always the result of poor choices. It often isn't—it's a consequence of life's unpredictable, uncontrollable events.

The Hidden Dangers of Scams and Financial Abuse

Scams don't just happen to the naive or uninformed. They prey on our most human vulnerabilities—compassion, loneliness, and trust. Elderly individuals and those who are lonely or emotionally fragile are particularly at risk.

One client that stands out is an elderly woman I knew through a friend. This woman's grandson was in college, and one day, she received a phone call. The caller pretended to be her grandson, claiming he was in trouble, in jail, and needed money immediately. "Don't call Mom," he said, playing on her desire to protect him. She wired $15,000, believing she was helping her grandson in a moment of crisis. But the scammers didn't stop there. They kept calling, spinning stories that led her to send more and more money. By the time the truth came out, she had lost $25,000—the entirety of her modest savings. For someone living on Social Security, this loss was catastrophic.

Financial abuse also falls under the umbrella of scams. Financial abuse frequently occurs in domestic violence situations, where control over money is used as a means of exerting power. If someone is being physically abused, there's a strong likelihood that they are also being financially manipulated. This type of abuse can involve restricting access to funds, taking out loans in the victim's name, or coercing them into financial decisions that are detrimental.

I've also seen this play out in households with drug addiction. I recall cases where parents used their adult children's Social Security numbers to open credit cards and buy drugs, ruining their children's credit and financial futures. Identity theft, even within families, is more common than most people think, and the consequences can be long-lasting.

Bankruptcy is designed not just for those who have mismanaged money but for those who have been manipulated, tricked, or caught in circumstances beyond their control. The shame and guilt that often accompany these situations can prevent people from seeking help, but please know that you're not alone and that solutions exist.

When Business Ventures Lead to Debt

I have filed bankruptcy for many small businesses over the years, from dog groomers to coffee shops to restaurants and lawn service providers. Most people don't realize that starting a small business typically means you, the owner, are personally signing off on loan documents, credit applications, and other financial commitments. And no, creating an LLC doesn't create an impenetrable shield between you and your business finances. If your business falters, you're still on the hook.

Take the case of one client, a young woman who inherited her mother's coffee shop, which happened to be a sinking ship weighed down by debt. The shop didn't own the property—it was leased—so what she truly gained was responsibility for rent, payroll, and the upkeep of the coffee shop's equipment. She poured her retirement savings into keeping it afloat. Her attachment to the shop was emotional; it was her mother's dream, not hers. She felt a duty to continue it, even as the financial strain became unbearable.

It wasn't until we sat down and had an honest conversation that she could see the whole picture. The truth was, her mother's business had been struggling long before she took it over, and it wouldn't become sustainable without significant changes beyond what she could afford. She needed to understand that it was okay to let go and that she wasn't obligated to sacrifice her financial future for a business that simply wasn't working. Bankruptcy, in her case, was the path to clarity and freedom.

Bankruptcy exists to allow people to take risks, fail, learn, and try again. It's why America celebrates stories like Walt Disney's. Before building an entertainment empire, Disney faced financial ruin and fell on his face. But he sure did it right the second time around. If you're a small business owner who finds yourself in overwhelming debt, know that seeking help isn't a defeat—it's a step toward reclaiming your entrepreneurial dreams. The lessons learned and the resilience gained can lead you to new, even greater ventures.

The Cycle of Overspending

When people think of overspending, they often picture someone indulging in shopping sprees or living beyond their means purely for the thrill of it. But in my experience, overspending as a primary cause of debt is tied to one of the other reasons you are in debt.

Overspending becomes a coping mechanism during times of financial or emotional stress. For example, suppose you are suddenly faced with the loss of a spouse who contributed to the household income. You might need groceries, medications, and other essentials. So, you turn to your credit card. The first time, it feels manageable—a temporary fix. But swiping that card becomes the only way to get by as days turn into weeks. Gas, food, and even medical co-pays start going on credit. Soon, it spirals out of control.

There are also lesser-known ways people use credit cards that blur the line between necessity and overspending. For example, in some states, a loophole allowed people to use store credit cards to buy Visa gift cards. People would then use these gift cards for groceries or gas to make ends meet when cash wasn't available. This kind of financial juggling reflects not carelessness but sheer survival instinct.

The trap of overspending often evolves into what I call the "robbing Peter to pay Paul" cycle. At this stage, most of a person's income is dedicated to making minimum payments, leaving them with no choice but to use credit for daily living expenses. The reliance on credit feeds the cycle of debt, with each purchase adding to balances that accrue interest at alarming rates. Before long, making those minimum payments becomes impossible under the weight of compounding interest. And the cycle continues...

Bankruptcy as a Lifeline

I want to offer a clear guideline that I've seen work time and time again. If you have $10,000 or more in unsecured, non-priority debt—think credit cards, medical bills, personal loans, payday loans—and you cannot create a budget that will allow you to pay it off in three years or less *without borrowing more money,* it's time to talk to a bankruptcy lawyer. If you're in a position where your debt feels like it's choking you and the numbers don't add up, it's NOT the time to dig deeper by borrowing against your 401(k), taking out a home equity line of credit, or doubling down on a consolidation loan. Those choices may seem like quick fixes, but they can leave you in a worse situation down the road. I often emphasize that this approach to bankruptcy can help people think of it as a responsible solution rather than a last resort.

When the wheels fall off the cart, emotional distress—whether it's anxiety, depression, or panic—impacts our ability to function in basic ways. Suddenly, even opening the mail feels impossible. This mental and emotional fog can act as a barrier to understanding what safe, legal options are available, like bankruptcy, that could actually offer relief. That's why I encourage people who are grieving or going through emotional upheavals to bring someone with them to our meetings—someone who can listen and help them process what's being said.

One of the most challenging aspects of my job is calming people down enough to see that while their grief or stress is valid, money is not emotional. You're allowed to cry over the loss of a loved one, but when it comes to finances, it's time to put on the gloves and approach the situation clinically and transparently. Separating emotions from financial problem-solving helps people refocus and regain a sense of control over their situation.

Throughout this chapter, we've explored how people find themselves trapped in debt—whether through job loss, medical emergencies, divorce, business failure, or even scams. The thread running through these situations is that debt happens *to* us. It's rarely the result of reckless spending or poor decision-making. Instead, it often begins with life events we cannot control, from a sudden health crisis to a transmission failure that leaves someone scrambling to make it to work the next day.

Most people don't walk into a payday lender with excitement; they do so because they're desperate and out of options. It's easy to judge from the outside and suggest that everyone should have emergency savings, comprehensive insurance, and perfect financial foresight. But the reality is different. Many people live paycheck to paycheck, one unforeseen expense away from financial chaos. Life is complex and often unforgiving, but knowing that help exists and there's a way out can be the first step to reclaiming your financial peace.

KEY TAKEAWAYS

➤ Debt often stems from uncontrollable life events, such as job loss, medical emergencies, the death of a spouse, or scams, not reckless behavior.

➤ Financial upheavals, like divorce or medical debt, frequently push individuals beyond their means, illustrating that debt can affect anyone regardless of careful planning.

➤ Overspending is often not simple indulgence but a survival mechanism triggered by financial or emotional stress, compounding debt issues over time.

➤ Bankruptcy can be a responsible step, not a failure. It offers relief, and a pathway to rebuild when repaying debt within a reasonable timeframe is impossible.

➤ Approaching financial problems with a clear, clinical mindset and seeking professional help can help people regain control and find peace during tough times.

CHAPTER FIVE

Strategies for Managing Debt

E very option sounds like a potential lifeline when you are in the thick of debt. But in reality, not all approaches to debt are created equal. Some may even worsen your situation. This chapter will guide you through the options, separating practical solutions from risky distractions so you can make informed choices.

Most solutions boil down to these seven main strategies:

1. Budgeting
2. Borrowing more money
3. Any form of debt settlement
4. Winning the lottery/inheriting money
5. Forgiveness programs
6. Dying
7. Talking to a bankruptcy lawyer

While all of these options are NOT necessarily safe, I urge you to be even more cautious of any debt solutions you see online or hear about that fall outside these categories. As I will explain, most of these seven options can worsen your problems, but anything outside these approaches is likely to be exceptionally risky and, very likely, fraudulent.

I often speak to one spouse who understands the seriousness of their family's debt situation but can not get their other half on board. Time and time again, the spouse reluctantly comes into the office or listens on speakerphone so they can hear what I'm saying. These skeptical spouses make the biggest turnaround once we go through the options. When they realize that there are only a few safe ways to manage debt, they suddenly start to understand the mistakes they've made up until now, and they're ready to lean into the possibility of true debt relief.

Building a Budget to Regain Control

I always advocate that a safe, responsible thing to do is start with budgeting. Creating a budget is one of the most powerful tools for gaining control over your finances. My colleague, Justin Brown-Woods, believes budgeting is a core step in tidying up your money management and financial journey. While it may not be a forever thing, and you certainly can't budget your way out of poverty, a budget is a very good middle ground for many.

Justin states, "When beginning a budget, we want to make sure people identify their income, expenses, and the time period in which we can work within those. Many budgets run month to month, but something like 90% (Bureau of Labor Statistics) are paid in different pay structures than monthly, so we have to identify when expenses go out and what the income is in that pay period.

Once we identify all of these numbers and include any debt payments, we can create the budget with the data. Our 'specialty' is value-based budgeting, so we highlight values for people and then budget accordingly, but a very common strategy to pair it with is zero-based budgeting, identifying every dollar you earn and giving it a role so that your budget is balanced to zero in each period.

Finally, once the budget is built, you must track expenses throughout the pay period. Tracking expenses means writing down when you spend money/pay bills to know where money is going. This is the KEY to successful budgeting. You can make all the beautiful budgets in the world, but if you don't track your expenses, you're just living on a hope and wish, and you have zero ability to reflect and grow. You should look back at previous spending each month and find trends/triggers highlighting struggles. If you do that, you can get ahead of those issues."

Justin and his wife Haley have a personal story from which they glean their expertise. Their journey wasn't easy; initially, it looked like they were headed for financial disaster. They received a substantial $600,000 payout from a lawsuit. Within just three and a half years, they had burned through all of it and accumulated an additional $225,000 in debt. Despite what looked like a financial catastrophe, Justin and Haley decided to take control rather than file for bankruptcy. They got serious about budgeting, setting firm financial goals, and reining in their spending.

In just 18 months, they reduced their debt from $225,000 to $130,000. Their discipline, honesty about their situation, and determination to tighten their belts were key factors in this turnaround.

Not only did they use budgeting as a tool to overcome their financial challenges, but they also launched a podcast to discuss their journey and promote honest conversations about money. Justin and Haley now help others by encouraging them first to attempt budgeting as a debt-management tool. And if budgeting isn't sustainable for some of their clients, they quickly recommend consulting a bankruptcy lawyer—knowing from their own experience how valuable that step can be. I agree that a bankruptcy lawyer is the next logical step when budgeting fails.

Justin and Haley's approach to financial recovery and commitment to guiding others reflect my values: empowering people to face debt without shame or embarrassment. They are a powerful example of resilience, proving that even the steepest financial obstacles can be overcome with the right mindset and tools.

Haley and Justin have a podcast called "The Price of Avocado Toast," where they share stories and advice from not only their own lives but also the lives of the people they help. They are a husband-and-wife financial coaching team that helps people learn how to budget, pay off debt, and spend in ways that bring them joy.

www.priceofavocadotoast.com
Justin Brown-Woods 707-953-0193

Borrowing to Manage Debt:
Proceed with Caution

Considering borrowing more money to manage existing debt? It's a strategy that can look appealing on the surface, but it's filled with potential pitfalls that could lead you further into financial trouble. When people consider borrowing, they're usually thinking about options like:

- Borrowing from a 401(k) or retirement plan
- Home equity line of credit
- Debt consolidation loan from a bank
- Short-term payday loans
- Credit cards or revolving credit

Each of these options comes with its own set of complexities, but they share a common risk: taking on new debt to handle old debt. I often compare giving more debt to someone with existing debt to giving alcohol to an alcoholic. Adding more isn't likely to solve the problem if you're already struggling with unsecured debt. Borrowing shifts balances from one place to another while the underlying debt grows, putting you in a riskier position.

One of the biggest mistakes I see is when people dip into retirement savings or home equity to pay off debt that could easily be discharged in bankruptcy. Retirement funds, for example, are 100% protected in all U.S. bankruptcies—why jeopardize them? Using your 401(k) puts vital resources at risk, often without solving the problem.

The same goes for home equity. Your home is your family's security, and risking it to cover credit card debt or medical bills just isn't worth it. These are exactly the kinds of unsecured, non-priority debts that bankruptcy was designed to eliminate, allowing you to keep your home and retirement savings intact.

Many people get trapped in a cycle of borrowing to deal with immediate issues without considering the long-term consequences. I've seen clients take out a home equity line of credit, thinking it would solve their debt problems, only to find themselves still needing to file for bankruptcy later. Now, they're left with depleted home equity and additional debt on their mortgage. In all of these situations, you're just moving pieces around the board without really getting anywhere.

The Pros and Cons of Debt Settlement

The marketing team who came up with the name "debt settlement" did an excellent job because the term makes everyone feel safe and gives the illusion they are doing something right. Though it may work for some, it's rarely the solution it's marketed to be for the following reasons:

- **No Legal Obligation for Creditors to Settle**: Unlike bankruptcy, which legally discharges debt, creditors are not required to accept debt settlement offers. Many people end up in situations where some creditors agree to settle while others refuse, resulting in lawsuits and wage garnishments.
- **Hidden Fees and Bait-and-Switch Tactics**: Many debt settlement companies engage in confusing practices, often misleading clients with "promises" that aren't entirely

transparent. A common tactic is setting up a debt settlement plan only to later switch it to a consolidation loan, leaving clients with more debt than they started with.

- **Risk of Lawsuits and Wage Garnishments**: Clients often mistakenly believe all their creditors are on board, only to be surprised by a lawsuit from a creditor not involved in the plan. The resulting wage garnishments can lead to financial instability and, in many cases, force clients to consider bankruptcy anyway.

- **No Reduction in Debt Principal**: In most cases, debt settlement doesn't actually reduce the principal debt. While it may slow or stop interest, it won't eliminate the core amount owed. By contrast, bankruptcy often stops interest accumulation and may discharge the principal entirely.

I recently had a client who had been paying $755 per month into a debt settlement plan for 11 months, totaling over $8,000. He believed this would keep all his creditors at bay. But after almost a year of payments, he was blindsided by a lawsuit from one of his creditors who wasn't part of the settlement agreement. Not only did he lose over $8,000, but he also lost nearly a year of time that could have been spent resolving his financial situation through bankruptcy. The lawsuit led to wage garnishment, forcing him to finally file for bankruptcy, which would have saved him time, money, and stress from the beginning.

Another client faced a similar issue with a debt settlement company that promised him a consolidated debt payment after he made consistent monthly payments. However, after six months, the debt settlement company switched him to a high-interest consolidation loan, adding even more debt. Despite his best efforts, he ended up filing for bankruptcy, as the debt settlement left him worse off financially.

Debt settlement can work, but only in specific circumstances:

- ➜ **Few Creditors**: If you have just one or two creditors, it's easier to confirm if they're truly participating in the settlement and to negotiate favorable terms.
- ➜ **Nonprofit Programs**: Nonprofit credit counseling agencies can sometimes offer legitimate programs that reduce interest rates and consolidate payments. While they don't reduce the principal, they can make repayment more manageable.
- ➜ **Professional Guidance**: Attorneys specializing in debt settlement and communicating directly with creditors can sometimes help clients achieve a more favorable outcome. However, having access to a lump sum to pay down debt is often necessary for success in this scenario.

For many, bankruptcy provides a more straightforward path out of debt. In Chapter 13 bankruptcy, for instance, all creditors are legally bound to the repayment plan, and interest on most debts stops accumulating. Most importantly, creditors are prohibited from suing, garnishing wages, or foreclosing on your property during the process. This court protection and the assurance of a legal resolution is something debt settlement companies cannot offer. The power they claim to have is often more about persuasion than actual results, leaving too many clients disappointed, frustrated, and still in debt. For those struggling to manage multiple creditors, the structure and protection of bankruptcy often provide a more reliable solution.

The Risk of Relying
on Inheritance to Pay Debt

While the idea of an inheritance serving as a financial lifeline may feel comforting, it's actually a risky and often unreliable plan. One of the primary challenges is the uncertainty of timing. Clients sometimes tell me they're counting on an inheritance to resolve their debt, but the truth is, none of us can predict when a loved one will pass away. Assuming that their passing will conveniently align with financial needs is ethically uncomfortable and practically unsound. Life has its own timeline; waiting for an event that may or may not occur at the right time is a volatile financial strategy. Even if someone is confident they will inherit, receiving those assets is not guaranteed. Family dynamics, unexpected expenses, or last-minute changes in a will can quickly alter the outcome.

If an inheritance does come through, any assets received are often at risk if there's outstanding debt. I've seen clients inherit family homes only to have creditors place liens on them because of unresolved debt. For those in significant debt, filing for bankruptcy now can clear out financial obligations, providing a clean slate so that when an inheritance does come, it's safe from creditors.

I had a client who was facing considerable debt but expected to inherit a substantial sum down the line. To prevent her future inheritance from being lost to creditors, we filed for bankruptcy to clear her debt. This gave her the ability to inherit without risking those assets.

However, there is an important rule in bankruptcy law to consider: any inheritance received within six months of filing becomes accessible to the bankruptcy court for debt repayment. For example, I once worked with a family where the client's elderly parent, who was in poor health, temporarily amended their will so that any inheritance during those six months would go to another family member. This minor, strategic adjustment protected the client's inheritance from creditors, allowing her to benefit later.

Combining debt management with inheritance planning is complex; this example highlights the importance of a proactive approach. Taking control of your debt today can ensure that, when the time comes, any inheritance truly benefits you rather than being siphoned off to repay creditors.

Bankruptcy as the Best Path Forward

1. Budgeting
2. Talking to a bankruptcy lawyer
3. Forgiveness programs

---

4. Borrowing more money
5. Any form of debt settlement
6. Winning the lottery/inheriting money
7. Forgiveness programs
8. Dying

Let's recap the list we were working from for this chapter. I've taken the liberty of reorganizing our debt relief options in order of importance and likelihood of success; this is the order in which I recommend you attack your unmanageable debt. As you can see, budgeting will always be the first option you should use.

But the point here is that there is a formula. Remember, there is a simple way to determine when bankruptcy is right for you:

If you have $10,000 of unsecured debt (bottom of the pyramid debt)

AND

You can NOT budget yourself out of your debt in 3 years or less WITHOUT borrowing more money,

THEN

You should talk to a bankruptcy lawyer

BEFORE you borrow more money,
BEFORE you cash out a 401(k)
BEFORE you go to a debt settlement company
BEFORE you take out a consolidation loan

When you're overwhelmed by debt, it's easy to be drawn to strategies that sound good but may actually work against you in the long run. Borrowing more money to solve debt rarely makes sense upon closer inspection—it's simply adding another layer to an existing problem. Similarly, debt settlement can often be dangerous and unregulated, and waiting for an inheritance is usually more fantasy than a viable plan.

The most reliable first step to managing debt is to create a budget. Budgeting provides a solid foundation and clarity, allowing you to track your spending and identify where to cut back. However, if budgeting alone isn't enough, remember that bankruptcy exists as a tool to help those who find themselves with unmanageable debt. Bankruptcy isn't about failure; it's a legal option designed to protect your most important assets—your home, retirement savings, and stability. Rather than circling around debt with consolidation loans or "solutions" that only move balances around, bankruptcy offers a clear path to reset and rebuild.

Gaining knowledge and understanding your options is what empowers you to make thoughtful decisions. You don't have to rush into bankruptcy, but consulting a bankruptcy lawyer early on gives you access to crucial information, helping you make informed choices based on a complete picture of your situation. Equipped with the right information, you can approach debt with a strategy that safeguards your future and brings genuine relief.

KEY TAKEAWAYS

➤ Not all debt solutions are created equal; focus on proven strategies and avoid anything that sounds too good to be true.

➤ Budgeting is a powerful tool for regaining control. It helps you track expenses, identify trends, and set realistic goals.

➤ Borrowing more to manage debt is risky and often shifts debt around without resolving underlying issues.

➢ Debt settlement may seem appealing, but it comes with hidden fees, unfulfilled promises, and legal risks that can lead to greater financial strain.

➢ Bankruptcy can be a viable option for unmanageable debt, offering a structured path to reset without risking assets like retirement savings and home equity.

CHAPTER SIX

The Bankruptcy Options

In this chapter, we're diving into the nuts and bolts of what bankruptcy is and what it can do for you. For the majority of people dealing with credit card debt, medical bills, personal loans, or even business-related debts, **Chapter 7** and **Chapter 13** are the main options. They offer different approaches to resolving financial challenges:

- **Chapter 7**: Often called a "liquidation bankruptcy," Chapter 7 focuses on wiping out unsecured debts like credit cards and medical bills. It's usually a faster process but may involve selling off non-exempt assets to pay creditors.
- **Chapter 13**: This is sometimes called a "reorganization bankruptcy." It allows you to create a repayment plan to pay off debts over three to five years while keeping your assets. It's ideal for individuals with a steady income who need a structured way to get back on track.

However, there are additional types of bankruptcy designed for specific circumstances:

- **Chapter 12**: This is a specialized bankruptcy for family farmers. Surprisingly, it also applies to small fish hatcheries! It functions similarly to Chapter 13.
- **Chapter 11**: Often associated with large business bankruptcies, Chapter 11 can also apply to consumers with substantial debt—though it's rare for everyday individuals to reach this threshold. As of June 2024, the debt limit for Chapter 11 dropped from over $1 million to about half a million dollars for unsecured debt like credit cards or personal loans. If you exceed this limit, Chapter 11 becomes your only option, as Chapter 13 isn't available to those with debt exceeding the cap.

Each type of bankruptcy carries its own responsibilities and expectations. By understanding what's available, you can make an informed decision about which path might be right for you—or if bankruptcy is even the right choice at all.

Note: The rules and thresholds around bankruptcy can change. For instance, the Chapter 11 debt limit adjustment in mid-2024 highlights how these regulations evolve. Always consult with a professional for the latest updates.

Everyone walking into a bankruptcy lawyer's office wants to qualify for Chapter 7. It's the simplest, cleanest option, and it lets you walk away from debt without a repayment plan. While many people might say, "I really want to pay my creditors back," the truth is, if you qualify to eliminate that debt entirely, most people will make that choice—and they should. It's often the right decision for saving yourself and moving forward.

However, not everyone has control over which type of bankruptcy they can file. There are very clear eligibility requirements for Chapter 7, and they involve two things: **your household income** and **your assets.** If either doesn't fit the guidelines, you might find yourself in Chapter 13 instead.

The Means Test: Household Income Limit

The Bankruptcy "Means Test" is one of the most significant factors in determining whether you qualify for Chapter 7 bankruptcy or if Chapter 13 is your only option. In simple terms, the Means Test is an income calculation that compares your household's earnings and expenses to a standard set by the federal government. It's designed to ensure that Chapter 7, which eliminates most debts outright, is reserved for those who genuinely can't afford to repay their creditors.

For example, let's say you're a single mom in Ohio with two kids. Ohio's income limit for a household of three is about $95,000 a year. That means if your income is on track to exceed $95,000, you won't qualify for Chapter 7. Instead, you'll need to consider Chapter 13.

Here's how the calculation works: the court looks back at your pre-tax income (gross income) for the six months before filing. So, if you file for bankruptcy on July 1, the court requires that you add all gross income from January 1 to June 30 earned by any eligible adult in your household. That six-month income total is then multiplied by two to determine whether you're below or above your state's Means Test limit. If you're above the threshold, Chapter 7 probably isn't an option for you.

The Means Test does not include any income paid under the Social Security Act, such as social security benefits, SSI, adoption subsidies paid through the SSA Act, etc. The only other income source excluded from your state's bankruptcy Means Test is VA benefits paid monthly to a veteran due to a disability.

The Means Test is nuanced and can play out differently for people living in different parts of the United States. For example, In Ohio, we have to include your adult son and their income if they live with you in your state's bankruptcy Means Test, but in other states, the way the "household size" is calculated can be wildly different.

If one spouse files for bankruptcy and the other does not, we can offset expenses using a "marital adjustment." This means we can subtract what a non-filing spouse still has to pay for their own debts and obligations as it depletes the total household income. It's important to understand that your state's Means Test will be unique to your jurisdiction, and you'll need a local bankruptcy lawyer to help you navigate it accurately.

Tackling the Means Test

When a client comes to me, the Means Test is one of the first things we work through. I ask for every pay stub from the past six months, and if their income is inconsistent, we create a detailed spreadsheet. We list every paycheck, record the gross income, and note all deductions. This process gives us an accurate average monthly income based on the past 180 days.

Many people are surprised by the numbers this process reveals. For instance, if someone is paid biweekly, they often assume they only receive two paychecks per month. But over six months, that occasional third paycheck in a month bumps their average income higher than they might expect. It's not always easy for clients to see their finances laid out so clearly—it can be an eye-opener.

Once we've calculated income, the next step is to factor in expenses. The Means Test uses a formula that incorporates standardized allowances for basic needs like housing, utilities, groceries, and healthcare. For example, the test might assume that $1,200 per month is sufficient for housing in Ohio. But if your actual mortgage is $1,500, that extra $300 can work in your favor by offsetting your income in the test.

However, the Means Test can feel frustratingly rigid. Many personal expenses that people consider essential, like a child's sports fees or other extracurricular activities, don't count. This can be a harsh reality for families. One client of mine learned this the hard way when her $700 monthly expense for her child's soccer team didn't factor into the test. It was a tough adjustment, but it highlighted an important truth: the Means Test isn't about luxuries or preferences—it's a forced budget focused solely on necessities.

At the end of this process, the Means Test spits out a number. If your income, after subtracting all approved expenses, is entirely consumed by your living costs, you "pass" the test. This green light allows you to file for Chapter 7. On the other hand, if there's any leftover income—what the test determines you can "afford" to pay—that amount is what you'd be required to contribute to a Chapter 13 repayment plan.

For example, if your household income is $117,000, but the limit in your state is $95,000, the Means Test will calculate how much you should be able to repay based on your expenses. That amount becomes the foundation for your Chapter 13 plan. While it might feel frustrating or even unfair, the goal of the test is to balance your absolute needs with what creditors are entitled to recover.

If the Means Test determines Chapter 13 is for you, it's not all bad news. The plan requires you to pay what the test says you can afford each month for five years. After that, any remaining debts are discharged, even if you didn't pay them in full. This means you're free from lingering financial burdens once you've fulfilled your obligation.

Some people in Chapter 13 end up paying 100% of their debts, but there are still benefits. It provides structured relief and protection from creditors while giving you the time and space to manage your finances.

The Asset Test and Your State's Bankruptcy Exemptions

Your assets are the second factor that can prevent you from filing Chapter 7. Chapter 7 is technically called a "liquidation bankruptcy," and this is where people tend to get nervous. They worry the court will take away their property—their home, their car, or other valuables. In theory, that could happen, but it doesn't have to. As bankruptcy lawyers, this is where we ensure your assets are protected. Note: In almost 30 years of practice, I've never had a client "lose a home" or a car (that they didn't want to get rid of).

Each state has specific bankruptcy exemptions that protect certain assets up to a particular value. For instance, your home equity and car value might be safe up to a certain amount, but filing Chapter 7 could put those assets at risk if your equity exceeds that limit. When this happens, we look at Chapter 13 as an alternative. Chapter 13 allows you to protect those assets while creating a repayment plan that works for you.

Everyone who comes to the table has debt, and everyone who comes to the table hopes to qualify for Chapter 7. But the reality is that the type of bankruptcy you file depends on the specifics of your financial situation. Whether you file Chapter 7 or Chapter 13, the goal is to help you handle overwhelming debt and give you the fresh start you need.

Why State Laws Matter in Bankruptcy

One of the most important things you need to know about bankruptcy is that while the laws are federal and set by Congress, their application varies significantly from state to state. There are two areas where these differences become clear: the **Means Test** and the **Asset Exemptions**. These variations can mean the difference between filing a Chapter 7 or a Chapter 13—or whether filing bankruptcy makes sense for you at all.

The Means Test, as we've discussed, is the income threshold that determines your eligibility for Chapter 7. However, those numbers are not uniform. They vary depending on the state and, in some cases, even the region within a state.

In Ohio, the income limit for a family of three is $95,000. That number will be different in Texas or Mississippi, and in New York, the limit is different between New York City and upstate New York. These differences account for regional variations in the cost of living, which means that where you live directly impacts passing the Means Test.

If you thought the Means Test was complicated, Asset Exemptions take it to another level. Exemptions determine how much of your property you're allowed to keep when filing for Chapter 7 bankruptcy. These exemptions are wildly different from state to state.

Let's look at Ohio as an example. In Ohio, the equity exemption for your home is $161,000 per person. That means if you're married, you and your spouse can protect up to $322,000 in equity in your home. For most people in Ohio, this means their homes are safe, even if they own them outright or have significant equity.

Now compare that to Illinois, where the home equity exemption is only $15,000. If you live in Illinois and your home is worth $85,000 with no mortgage, you wouldn't be able to file Chapter 7 because your equity exceeds the exemption by $70,000. Filing Chapter 7 would mean the court could sell your home to pay creditors. In this case, you'd have no choice but to file Chapter 13, where you'd pay back the $70,000 of unprotected equity over a three- to five-year repayment plan.

And then there's Texas. Texas has no limit on home or vehicle exemptions. You could own a $10 million mansion and a luxury car like a Bugatti, be on Social Security, pass the Means Test, and keep everything. Meanwhile, someone in Illinois with a $85,000 house might lose it in bankruptcy.

These state-by-state differences highlight why working with an experienced bankruptcy lawyer in your area is so important. If you live in a state with low exemptions, like Illinois, there may be better solutions than bankruptcy, especially if you want to protect your home. But you could have more flexibility if you live in a state like Texas or Ohio. Two people with identical debts and assets could face completely different outcomes simply because they live in different states.

You Have Options

Recently, I sat down with a woman whose story I often hear — she was overwhelmed, scared, and feeling like there was no way out. She and her husband lived alone and were caught in a financial spiral. Their combined household income was over $90,000, which meant she didn't qualify for Chapter 7 bankruptcy under Ohio's limit of about $74,000 for a two-person household. And because bankruptcy is a household income test, we had to include her husband's income, even though he wasn't the one filing.

When I explained that Chapter 7 wasn't an option for her, the weight of that reality hit her hard.

The first question I asked was, "How much credit card debt do you have?"

Her answer: "$38,000."

The second question: "What are you paying in minimum payments right now?"

She hesitated, unsure. "I don't know, maybe $1,000?"

"Let's dig into this," I said. "Pull up your bank account, and let's look at what's really going on."

Piece by piece, she started rattling off numbers: $400 here, $600 there, another $350, and then another $300. By the time we tallied it all up, she was paying between $1,600 and $1,800 a month—just on minimum payments. If she continued down that road, it would take her 22 years to pay off the debt; twenty-two years of sending every spare dollar to the credit card companies and barely making a dent, thanks to the relentless grip of compounding interest.

This is where bankruptcy changes everything. After running the numbers and going through the options, we found a solution: Chapter 13. Instead of paying $1,600 to $1,800 a month for 22 years, she could pay less than $900 a month for just five years—and walk away debt-free. Compounding interest stops the moment you enter Chapter 13. That's the trap most people don't realize they're in. When you're only making minimum payments, the interest piles up so fast that even decades of payments barely scratch the surface of the underlying debt. But in bankruptcy, that cycle ends.

At first, she resisted. She didn't want to file for bankruptcy. Like so many others, she saw it as a last resort, something to be ashamed of. She had come to me in tears, desperate because her wages had just started getting garnished, but still clinging to the hope that there might be another way.

As we talked, reality began to sink in. Bankruptcy wasn't something to fear—it was a tool that could give her the freedom to live her life again. By the end of our conversation, her tears had shifted from hopelessness to relief.

Her plan is now set. She'll pay less than $800 a month in Chapter 13, and in five years, her $38,000 in credit card debt will be gone. For the first time in years, she'll have breathing room. Instead of scrambling to keep up with crushing payments, she can start saving, rebuilding, and living her life without the shadow of debt looming over her.

Misunderstanding bankruptcy can keep people trapped in financial misery for years—or even decades. She thought she had no choice but to keep paying, but when she finally reached out for help, she discovered a better option. Now, she had the chance to rebuild her future. Sometimes, the hardest part is making that first call. But once you do, everything can change.

Whether you qualify for Chapter 7 or need the structure and protection of Chapter 13, the most important takeaway is this: **you have options.** As you navigate your own situation, remember that the first step toward freedom is asking the right questions. Take what you've learned here, talk to an experienced lawyer, and begin to shape a future where debt no longer defines you.

KEY TAKEAWAYS

➢ Bankruptcy offers tailored solutions, with Chapter 7 providing fast relief through liquidation of unsecured debts or Chapter 13 offering a structured repayment plan to keep assets.

➢ Eligibility for Chapter 7 depends on income and asset thresholds, which vary by state and can significantly impact your options.

➤ The Means Test evaluates income and expenses to determine whether you qualify for Chapter 7 or need to pursue Chapter 13, which balances necessities with creditor repayment.

➤ State-specific exemptions play a role in what assets you can protect, making local legal guidance essential.

➤ Bankruptcy is a tool, not a failure—it can stop the debt cycle, provide relief, and light the way to financial freedom.

CHAPTER SEVEN

The Process and Timeline for Filing Bankruptcy

The journey becomes much more manageable when you know what to expect from the bankruptcy process. From your initial consultation to the final hearings, I'll cover everything here to help you feel prepared and confident.

The Initial Consultation

You typically begin with an initial consultation with a bankruptcy attorney. Most attorneys still offer free consultations, though some have started charging due to increased caseloads and demand. If offered a free consultation, these sessions are often brief, lasting about 20 minutes. For individuals with complex financial situations, such as owning multiple properties or businesses, it's a good idea to communicate these details upfront. Some attorneys may extend the consultation time for a fee or schedule a longer appointment to address your specific concerns.

During this meeting, your attorney will evaluate your situation, discuss your options, and guide you on the next steps. Whether the consultation takes place in person, by phone, or over Zoom depends on your region and the lawyer's preference.

Preparing for Your Consultation

Preparation is key to making your consultation productive. Gather necessary financial documents and information beforehand. Your attorney will need details about your income, assets, and debts. This includes recent pay stubs for not just you but for all the adults in your household, a list of vehicles and properties you own, their estimated values, and the balances on any loans tied to them. Tools like Kelley Blue Book or Zillow can help estimate the value of your assets, and checking your mortgage balance online ensures accurate figures.

It's also helpful to clearly understand your family's overall financial picture. Some attorneys may provide forms for you to fill out before the meeting, saving time and ensuring your consultation is thorough. Being organized and prepared helps your lawyer assess whether bankruptcy is viable for you and which chapter—Chapter 7 or Chapter 13—is most appropriate.

Understanding the Costs

Filing for bankruptcy involves several costs that should be factored into your decision. Depending on your region and court requirements, attorney fees for a Chapter 7 bankruptcy typically range from $1,750 to $4,000. Additionally, there is a court filing fee of approximately $340. Since the 2005 overhaul of bankruptcy laws, you will also need to complete two mandatory financial courses, which are quick and can usually be done online or by phone.

The **credit counseling course** must be completed before filing for bankruptcy. This step is non-negotiable, as a certificate of completion must be attached to your bankruptcy petition when submitted to the court. The certificate is only valid for six months. If you take the course but don't file within that time frame, you'll need to retake it. The credit counseling class aims to help individuals assess their financial situation and explore alternatives to bankruptcy, though the decision to file has already been made for many.

The second requirement, the **financial management course**, takes place after filing but must be completed before your case is discharged. This course focuses on basic financial skills like budgeting and managing credit.

Both courses are straightforward to complete. Not-for-profit agencies offer them, so the cost is minimal, and many bankruptcy lawyers include the fees for these classes in their overall legal charges. For those filing due to catastrophic events, such as a failed business or overwhelming medical expenses, the classes may seem unnecessary—no amount of budgeting can reverse a major financial disaster. However, the courses can provide valuable insights for others who struggle with day-to-day money management.

The good news is that these classes aren't difficult or time-consuming. They're designed to be accessible to everyone, so there's no need to worry about them being a barrier to completing the bankruptcy process.

The Importance of Timing

Your lawyer will consider factors like your income, assets, and even your pay periods to determine the optimal time to file. For example, individuals with fluctuating incomes, such as seasonal workers, may need to wait until their average income qualifies them for Chapter 7 bankruptcy.

Remember, the Means Test uses a six-month lookback to calculate eligibility. As a lawyer, there are a lot of nuances relative to the timing of filing your bankruptcy. The nice thing about a 6-month average is that it can change more quickly than if we had to use a one-year average. What if you were a construction worker, but most of your earnings were from March to October? If you wanted to file in October, we'd go 6 months backward and get a larger chunk of your income than if you waited until late winter to file. If you're close to the Means Test, I would probably want you to file bankruptcy in January or February because you'll be more likely to pass the Means Test. If you don't pass it by then, your Chapter 13 bankruptcy payment will be calculated using the lower 6-month numbers.

Imagine you got a $10,000 bonus at Christmastime. If you're close to the Means Test, waiting to file bankruptcy after July makes sense. If we have an additional $10k in your 6-month lookback, that number will be doubled, making it look like you have more income than you actually do.

Part of the art of being a bankruptcy lawyer is helping you weigh the timing of your filing. Sometimes, waiting a few months until your average income decreases could make you eligible for a

Chapter 7. Similarly, filing just before payday ensures your bank account balance is at its lowest, avoiding potential complications. Lawyers understand how to maximize bankruptcy to help you the most.

Navigating the Paperwork

One of the most challenging aspects of filing for bankruptcy is gathering and organizing the required paperwork. This often causes delays as people second-guess their decisions or procrastinate. But completing this step is your ticket to financial freedom.

Think of the cost and effort involved in bankruptcy as an investment in your future. While paying attorney fees and gathering paperwork may feel burdensome, these steps are necessary to secure a fresh financial start. Your lawyer will help you stay on track and ensure all required documents are in order.

What to Expect After Filing

Once your bankruptcy is filed, everything moves quickly. Within 30 to 45 days, you'll attend a bankruptcy hearing with a trustee assigned to your case. While the idea of a hearing can be intimidating, it's a routine part of the process designed to ensure fairness and transparency.

I often compare bankruptcy hearings to a trip to the BMV (Bureau of Motor Vehicles) to renew your driver's license. It's not exactly pleasant, and you might see a lot of grumpy faces. You might also worry about whether you have the right paperwork or whether everything will go smoothly. But just like renewing your license, bankruptcy is a bureaucratic process, not a judgment of your character or decisions.

During the hearing, a trustee will oversee your case. These trustees are independent contractors appointed by the United States Department of Justice. Their job is to act on behalf of your creditors to verify that your bankruptcy petition is accurate, lawful, and complete. They focus on three main areas:

- **Confirming Your Identity:** The trustee will verify your identity, often by comparing your photo ID to your appearance during a Zoom or in-person hearing.
- **Checking for Fraud:** They review your paperwork to ensure you haven't hidden assets or misrepresented your financial situation. For example, failing to disclose a property in another state would be considered fraud.
- **Evaluating Non-Exempt Assets:** Trustees determine whether any of your assets fall outside your state's exemption protections. If unprotected assets are found, they may be liquidated to pay your creditors, with the trustee receiving a portion of the proceeds.

For Chapter 7 cases, the hearing is typically straightforward and less intensive. Chapter 13 hearings, on the other hand, involve more detailed discussions about your repayment plan. You have nothing to fear if you've been honest, provided complete information, and worked with an experienced attorney. A good lawyer will have reviewed your assets and exemptions thoroughly, ensuring there are no surprises during the hearing.

How Long Will All of This Take?

The truth is that the timeline often depends on how quickly you can gather the required paperwork and secure the funds to hire a bankruptcy lawyer. These are the most common barriers for many people, but being proactive can make all the difference. Preparing beforehand ensures you're ready to act before your financial circumstances become critical, such as wage garnishments or frozen bank accounts.

Take, for example, the story of a teacher I recently worked with. He earned a good salary—nearly $90,000 a year—but had been struggling with garnished wages for three months. He thought that was the worst of it until he tried to put gas in his car one day and discovered creditors had completely wiped out his bank account. Suddenly, he had no way to access his money for basic necessities.

The teacher admitted he had seen the signs and had plenty of lead time to consult a bankruptcy lawyer, but he kept putting it off. By the time he reached out, he was desperate. Coming up with the funds to pay for a lawyer and file for bankruptcy became even harder because his resources were drained.

I encourage people to act before desperation sets in because the day you file is the day you reclaim your peace of mind. Take this step confidently, knowing that you are not alone and have the tools, support, and knowledge to come out stronger on the other side!

KEY TAKEAWAYS

➤ Begin the bankruptcy process with an initial consultation, ensuring you are well-prepared with detailed financial documents to maximize the session's effectiveness.

➤ Understand the costs and requirements, including attorney fees, court filing fees, mandatory credit counseling, and financial management courses.

➤ Timing is critical when filing bankruptcy, with factors like income fluctuations and account balances playing a significant role in determining eligibility and maximizing benefits.

➤ Gather and organize all required paperwork promptly to avoid delays, viewing the effort as an investment in securing a fresh financial start.

➤ Filing is the first step toward reclaiming peace of mind, supported by experienced attorneys and a structured process designed to guide you through challenging times and toward a stronger financial future.

PART THREE

Life After Debt

CHAPTER EIGHT

What to Expect After Filing Bankruptcy

W e've talked about the big picture—why bankruptcy exists and how it works—but now it's time to get practical. What happens after you file? What steps should you anticipate? This chapter is about giving you clarity. Knowing what to expect from the moment you file to the day your case is resolved does three important things:

- **Empowers You**: You'll feel equipped to handle the process.
- **Builds Confidence**: You'll approach each step with more ease and less anxiety.
- **Enables Self-Advocacy**: You'll know what questions to ask and how to interact with your attorney effectively.

One of my goals is to help you become a better consumer of legal services. Many people hesitate to ask questions when talking to a lawyer. I want you to feel confident enough to ask anything. By understanding the process, you can have more meaningful conversations with your attorney and ensure you're getting the help you deserve. If something doesn't look or feel right as you go through bankruptcy, you'll know. And when you know, you can take action.

Dispelling Myths About Life After Bankruptcy

What Really Happens to Your Credit Score

One of the biggest fears about bankruptcy is its impact on credit scores. Many believe it will destroy their financial future, leaving them in a world where they can never recover. But the truth is much more hopeful—and often surprising.

I've seen countless people walk into my office with credit scores they consider high. These are hardworking individuals, often maintaining a score above 700 while juggling minimum payments on significant debt. But what they don't realize is that their credit score is a fragile illusion—artificially inflated by a constant cycle of robbing Peter to pay Paul. Think of bankruptcy as a chance to rebuild your credit. Yes, there's an initial drop for some people, but for many, especially those already struggling, bankruptcy can actually improve their credit score! While people with high credit scores can expect a drop, if your credit score is under 580, filing bankruptcy will do the heavy lifting to pull it up into the high 500s or low 600s.

Let me tell you about a client I worked with recently. She was on Social Security, earning $1,800 a month, and living in her family home—a modest property worth about $80,000, with only $7,000 left on her mortgage. On paper, her situation seemed manageable. Her credit score was over 750.

But she was drowning in $38,000 of credit card debt. She was making minimum payments on time, but it came at the expense of everything else. When her home needed a new roof, she discovered that her seemingly great credit score didn't mean she could borrow what she needed. Her debt-to-income ratio had tipped too far, and lenders saw her as a risk. She felt trapped. If she didn't take action, her credit score would start to slip. And without access to financing, maintaining her home—or her peace of mind—would become impossible.

We filed a Chapter 7 bankruptcy. Her credit score dropped, but only to about 610. That drop, while scary for some, became her starting point. Her debt was erased, giving her room to breathe. Now, she's on a path to rebuild her credit, and within a year, she'll likely qualify for a home equity line of credit. This means she can finally replace her roof and maintain her home, something that felt impossible before bankruptcy.

What would have happened if she'd clung to the myth of her "perfect" credit score? She'd still be stuck in a cycle of financial instability with no real way out. Bankruptcy wasn't the end for her—it was the beginning of a better, more stable financial future.

Rebuilding your credit after bankruptcy is simple but requires consistency. I encourage you to learn the financial system's rules and use them to your advantage. Ask yourself:

- *How can I secure a credit card within months of filing?*
- *What steps will take me to a 720 credit score in a year or two?*
- *How do I avoid accumulating unnecessary debt again?*

These aren't mysteries—they're manageable steps anyone can follow. The process isn't difficult, but it does demand discipline.

Financing a Car...Surprisingly Easy!

Buying a car after filing for bankruptcy is often one of the easiest financial steps to take. I've seen it firsthand, time and time again. Car financing doesn't rely solely on your credit score. It's about your ability to make payments, which comes down to income and savings. For my clients who meet certain income thresholds—single earners making $3,500 a month or households earning $4,000 or more—there are lenders specifically designed to work with people emerging from bankruptcy.

Let me share an example. I work with a car dealership that exclusively serves people in or coming out of bankruptcy. To even visit this dealership, you need a referral from a bankruptcy attorney—that's how committed they are to helping people rebuild.

Here's what makes their approach different:

- **Used Cars with Full Warranties**: Every car comes with a bumper-to-bumper warranty, ensuring reliability.
- **Short Loan Terms**: Payments are structured for four years or less, preventing long-term negative equity.
- **Mandatory GAP Insurance**: This protects you if the car's value drops below what you owe, a common issue for those with previous financial struggles.

This dealership is just one example of an entire network of industries built to support people after bankruptcy. From cars to credit cards to housing, there are resources designed to help you move forward, not hold you back.

One concern I often hear is, "But won't I pay sky-high interest rates?" It's a valid question, but even a low interest rate isn't necessarily saving you money if you're trading in a car with negative equity. Let me give you a real-world example: I had a client who had a 2016 Honda Civic worth $10,000, but she still owed $20,000. My client wanted to "keep it" because the loan was only 4% interest. But what does a 4% interest on a car mean? Well, my client had three years left to pay on the $20,000 she still owed, and her monthly payment would remain $590/month. Over the next three years, my client would pay the underlying $20,000, and she would pay $1,257 in interest. That means she would end up paying $21,257 for her own 2016 Honda Civic worth $10,000!

But if my client surrendered her $10,000 Honda Civic, she could turn around and finance a different 2016 Honda Civic for $10,000. Even if her interest rate were 20% on her "newer" 2016 Honda Civic, her payment would be $371.64 a month for three years, and she'll pay a total of $3,378 in interest. That means my client will pay $13,378 for a 2016 Honda Civic. And if my client had $590/month to spend, she could get into a $16,000 Honda Civic that's at least four years newer.

As you can see, a "newer" car with a higher interest rate is almost always a smarter financial choice than keeping a car with negative equity, even if the interest rate on the newer car is high.

And remember, once you've filed for bankruptcy, your credit score starts climbing. Within six months, it could jump from 620 to 700 or higher. That's when you refinance your car loan for a better rate. The process works—it just takes a bit of time.

Buying a Home

Buying a home after bankruptcy isn't usually a right-away move like getting a car might be—but it's absolutely possible. In fact, many of my clients qualify for a mortgage within two to four years of filing, especially when they take intentional steps to rebuild their credit and financial habits.

Yes, you read that right! If you filed Chapter 7 bankruptcy, you could be eligible for an FHA loan or a VA loan just two years after discharge, as long as you've worked to re-establish credit and can explain the circumstances that led to your bankruptcy. This includes things like job loss, medical bills, or divorce—life events that are often out of your control.

If you're aiming for a conventional mortgage (through lenders backed by Fannie Mae or Freddie Mac), the typical waiting period is four years after a Chapter 7 discharge. However, some lenders may approve you sooner—after just two years—if you can document extenuating circumstances.

If you filed Chapter 13, the timeline can actually be shorter. After just 12 months of on-time payments under your repayment plan, you may be eligible for an FHA or VA mortgage—with court approval. Once your Chapter 13 is complete and discharged, you'll typically wait:

- Two years for a conventional loan
- Or four years if your case was dismissed without completion

In short, bankruptcy doesn't block homeownership. It just pushes the timeline a bit—and with the right steps, that timeline is shorter than most people think.

Four Truths About Life After Bankruptcy

Here are four incredible opportunities my clients often discover after filing:

- ★ **Financing a New Car**: Many of my clients can finance a reliable, fully warranted car the day after we file.
- ★ **Accessing Credit Cards**: Within weeks, they often qualify for new, zero-balance credit cards.
- ★ **Rebuilding Scores**: Credit scores typically climb back to 720 within 12-18 months.
- ★ **Qualifying for a Home Loan**: Within 2-4 years, many clients can finance a home.

Understanding the Impact on Co-Signers and Co-Borrowers

A commonly misunderstood aspect of bankruptcy involves how it affects co-signers and co-borrowers. These terms are often used interchangeably, but they're different. Being a co-signer is one of the riskiest financial positions you can take. As a co-signer, you're legally obligated to pay the debt if the primary borrower defaults, but you don't own the asset tied to the loan. Think about it: the person you're co-signing for likely has poor credit—otherwise, they wouldn't need a co-signer. That alone should be a red flag.

If you co-sign for your child's car loan, you're on the hook for the payments but don't own the car. You can't sell it to mitigate the loss if the payments aren't made. Worse, lenders don't notify co-signers when payments are missed, so you might not even realize there's a problem until it's too late.

If you're the co-signer and the primary borrower files bankruptcy, the lender will come after you for the entire debt. It's as though the primary borrower simply stopped paying. You'll be responsible for the remaining balance, and if the asset is repossessed, you're still liable for the unpaid portion after the lender sells it.

If you're the one filing bankruptcy, the outcome depends on the primary borrower's behavior:

If the Primary Borrower Continues Payments:

- Your bankruptcy removes your obligation to the loan, but the primary borrower can keep the asset and maintain the loan as long as they make timely payments.
- For example, let's say you co-signed for your daughter's car loan. If she keeps making payments, she gets to keep the car. The loan essentially transitions to her sole responsibility without adverse effect on her payment terms.

If the Primary Borrower Defaults:

- In this case, the lender may repossess the asset and pursue the primary borrower for the unpaid balance. If both of you are struggling with the loan, you may both need to file bankruptcy.

Filing bankruptcy can actually be a strategic way to remove yourself as a co-signer. If you're tied to a loan where you have no control—like a car loan for someone else—your bankruptcy filing eliminates your liability for that debt.

For example, if you're a co-signer on your daughter's car loan, your bankruptcy essentially erases your responsibility. As long as she continues making the payments, nothing changes for her. But if she stops paying, the lender can only go after her, not you.

Unlike co-signers, co-borrowers have more control because their names are on the title of the asset. If you're a co-borrower, you have ownership rights and can sell the asset if payments aren't being made.

If you're considering co-signing a loan for someone, explore becoming a co-borrower instead. It might feel awkward to ask, but it gives you much more power to protect yourself financially.

Climbing Out of the Hole

One of the most persistent myths about bankruptcy is that it leaves you with insurmountable long-term financial challenges. That couldn't be further from the truth. In fact, the real danger lies in not addressing your debt. The consequences of staying trapped in unmanageable financial situations far outweigh those of filing for bankruptcy.

Let me share an analogy I use with my clients when they're overwhelmed by what bankruptcy means:

Imagine you're sliding down into a deep, dark hole. It's terrifying. There's nothing to grab onto, no sunlight, and you feel completely lost. Bankruptcy does three things:

1. **It Stops the Fall**: Bankruptcy puts a solid floor beneath you. You're no longer sliding deeper into debt.
2. **It Lifts You Up**: The process raises you high enough to see the light. You're still in the hole but can see the world around you again.
3. **It Throws You a Rope**: Bankruptcy gives you a way out—a rope to climb back into the financial world.

Here's where people diverge:

1. **Most People Start Climbing** by grabbing the rope and figuring out how to climb out step by step. Some are faster, others slower, but they're moving up.
2. **Some Stay in the Hole**: They decide they're content. They don't need credit or financial engagement. These are the people who metaphorically pitch a tent, roast hot dogs, and enjoy the peace of simply existing.
3. **A Few Start Digging**: Unfortunately, some people break through the floor bankruptcy gave them, digging themselves deeper into debt and sliding back down.

The choice is yours. Most of my clients climb the rope. They might not all do it the same way or at the same speed, but they're determined to reach the top. The magic of bankruptcy is that it gives you the chance to rewrite your financial story, and if you're willing to climb the rope, you'll find that wonderful things await in the light!

KEY TAKEAWAYS

➤ While bankruptcy may initially lower your credit score, it often creates opportunities for rapid improvement and better financial options within months.

➤ Financing significant purchases like cars and homes is achievable post-bankruptcy, with tailored resources and strategies to support recovery.

➤ Co-signing and co-borrowing have distinct financial implications; understanding and addressing them through bankruptcy can protect your financial future.

➤ The real power of bankruptcy lies in taking action to climb out of debt. It offers a path to rewriting your financial story and moving toward brighter opportunities.

CHAPTER NINE

Rebuilding and Embracing Your Financial Future

You've come a long way. You've faced challenges, made sacrifices, and shown courage in the face of what might have felt like insurmountable odds. Now, it's time to focus on embracing a financial future that feels safe and secure. Whether rebuilding your credit score, reestablishing healthy financial habits, or laying a foundation for career success, the tools and strategies here will help you create a life that works for you and your family—on your terms. Your dreams, no matter how big or bold, are still attainable.

The good news is it's not rocket science. With some discipline and simple steps, getting back to a 720 credit score is absolutely achievable. The process isn't complicated; it just requires consistency:

- **Pay attention to your finances**: Know where your money is going and prioritize your needs.

- **Make small changes**: Small, consistent actions—like paying bills on time—have a big impact over time.
- **Commit to discipline**: You don't need to overhaul your life; you just need to stay steady in your efforts.

Turning Bankruptcy into a New Beginning

With very few exceptions, bankruptcy creates a scenario where all things become possible. I often think about the clients I've helped and the remarkable transformations they've achieved after making the brave decision to file. If I could, I'd parade my clients in a celebratory line in front of my office, and I know most of them would proudly say, "Filing for bankruptcy was the best decision we ever made. We wish we'd done it sooner!"

One story that stands out involves close friends of mine. Though I've changed some details to protect their privacy, the essence of their journey remains the same. They were newly married—a young, disciplined, and organized couple who had their lives meticulously planned out. They envisioned their future clearly: a baby after one year, a second child at the three-year mark, strategic use of PTO for vacations, and careful savings to ensure everything went smoothly.

Life, however, had other plans.

Two months after the birth of their first child, they received shocking news: she was pregnant again—this time with twins. The news was neither expected nor joyful. The pregnancy came with complications, and she ended up on bed rest. The twins were born prematurely, requiring extended medical treatment and care.

Both parents were forced to step away from work, and their carefully constructed plans began to crumble. They found themselves broken, terrified, and ashamed without the resources to handle this upheaval. They felt an overwhelming sense of failure.

But they had the strength to reach out to me. Admitting they needed help took immense courage, but that one decision changed everything. We sat down together, and I helped them craft a plan. The first step was filing a straightforward Chapter 7 bankruptcy. At the time, they were upside down on their car loan and their real estate—both financial burdens we were able to eliminate through the process. The bankruptcy wiped out their debt and gave them a clean slate. They could finally breathe again, free from the crushing weight of their financial struggles.

Fast forward to today, and their story is one of incredible success. All three of their children are now in college, thriving and building their futures. She is working in a lucrative field, earning an impressive income, while he is a respected professor. They are admired in their community, popular among their peers, and well-loved by everyone who knows them. Most people in their lives don't even know they filed for bankruptcy. The stigma they once feared never materialized because bankruptcy didn't define them—it freed them.

The Role of Financial Literacy in Your Fresh Start

Financial literacy is the toolset that allows you to make informed decisions, avoid past mistakes, and build a life of stability and growth. And yet, for something so critical, it is rarely taught effectively.

Our education system isn't keeping up when it comes to teaching financial literacy. While some states are beginning to mandate it, the curriculum is outdated, clunky, and far from engaging. It's not helping people navigate the complexities of modern financial systems or the rapidly changing laws.

This lack of education starts at home. Parents, who are often overwhelmed and stretched thin, can't teach what they were never taught themselves. Financial misinformation becomes a cycle, passed down like a game of telephone, with outdated and incorrect advice being perpetuated across generations.

Contrary to common misconceptions, people rarely file for bankruptcy more than once. In my experience, clients who go through bankruptcy leave with a deeper understanding of finances than most people walking down the street. Bankruptcy is like a crash course in financial literacy. You learn about budgeting, debt management, and the importance of credit in ways that stay with you.

The bankruptcy process can be life-changing, especially for those who approach it with bravery, an open mind, and a willingness to embrace the opportunities it provides. When one of my clients adopted this mindset, he transformed his financial habits and set himself on a path to long-term stability.

When he first came to me, his financial situation was dire. He was upside down on a car loan, constantly juggling bills, and trapped in the exhausting cycle of robbing Peter to pay Paul. Bankruptcy was his last resort, but instead of treating it as an ending, he saw it as a new beginning. He shared his plan—a clear roadmap to financial independence.

His first move was to let go of his expensive car. He scraped together $2,500 to buy a very cheap, used car, which he planned to drive for as long as possible. What was truly inspiring was what he decided to do next.

Instead of falling back into old habits, he committed to financial discipline. The $599 he had been paying monthly for his previous car loan was redirected into a savings account. His goal? To save enough money to make a substantial down payment on a newer, used car when his current car eventually gave out.

He planned to:

→ **Save consistently**: Build up $3,000–$5,000 for a down payment.
→ **Buy smart**: Purchase a used car and pay it off within two to three years.
→ **Repeat the cycle**: Continue saving the equivalent of his car payment to prepare for the next vehicle purchase, ensuring he would never be upside down on a car loan again.

But he didn't stop there. Recognizing the freedom bankruptcy had given him, he took half of what he had previously paid toward credit card minimums and redirected it into another savings account. This fund was earmarked for a new goal: starting a business. With a five-year plan now in place, he is focused on achieving financial independence.

What made this story so powerful was his thoughtful approach. He didn't just react to his circumstances; he chose to be proactive to ensure he would never return to the financial hardships he faced before bankruptcy. This level of clarity and discipline isn't something everyone achieves, but it's a testament to what's possible when you embrace financial literacy and take full advantage of the fresh start bankruptcy offers.

Small Wins Lead to Big Success

Rebuilding your financial life after overcoming debt starts with one essential principle: **start small.** Set achievable goals, celebrate small victories, and steadily build toward your dreams.

Let's go back to the story of the gentleman with the car. His first goal was simple: purchase a $2,500 car that would serve him reliably for at least ten months. His second goal was to save $5,000–$6,000 while driving that car, so he could make a substantial down payment on a better vehicle. From there, he planned to pay off the newer car as quickly as possible and continue saving for the next one, ensuring he would never be upside down on a car loan again.

This approach—setting small, specific, and winnable goals—allowed him to gain momentum and confidence. It's a strategy that works for anyone looking to rebuild their financial stability.

Before setting your goals, ask yourself: *"What am I trying to achieve?"*

Are you saving for a down payment on a house? Planning for retirement? Dreaming of launching the next big tech startup? The scope of your goals will shape your plan. Whatever your ambition, make sure your goals are realistic and attainable. Avoid setting yourself up for failure by aiming for something impossible quickly, like earning a million dollars in two years. Instead, focus on small, progressive steps that will move you toward your ultimate vision.

A coach once told me, "Set rules for yourself that you can win." If your rules are too strict, you'll fail and face unnecessary disappointment. Be honest with yourself about what you can commit to, and remember—you're the judge of your own life.

For example:

- Pay your bills on time every month.
- Use credit responsibly to rebuild your score.
- Learn the difference between good debt (like a mortgage) and bad debt (like revolving credit card debt).

These small habits may seem simple, but they are powerful building blocks for a stable financial future.

Discipline in your daily spending is crucial, but it's only half the battle. The other half is looking ahead and preparing for the unexpected. Life is unpredictable—job loss, illness, economic downturns, or personal tragedies like divorce or the death of a spouse can derail even the best-laid plans.

Finances are like chess, not checkers. Always think several moves ahead:

- **Anticipate risks**: Set aside funds for emergencies and insure yourself against major financial setbacks.
- **Plan for long-term goals**: Build retirement savings, create a cushion for your family's future, and consider how you'll adapt to life's inevitable changes.

The biggest financial challenge most people face isn't a lack of money. It's a lack of discipline and awareness. When you can master both, you'll be in control of your finances. Remember, small, thoughtful actions today can lead to significant victories tomorrow.

As we conclude this chapter and the book, I want to leave you with one vital message: **bankruptcy is here to help you.**

In a world that often feels unsafe, chaotic, and confusing, bankruptcy stands as one of the only safe and legal ways to manage unsecured debt and forge a pathway to stability. If you've made it this far, whether you've read every word or skimmed for the highlights, you've already taken an important step. By picking up this book, you've shown an openness to learning, a willingness to accept change, and a desire to put safeguards in place for your financial future.

The other side of bankruptcy is brighter than you can imagine. It's a place where fear gives way to confidence, chaos is replaced by clarity, and new possibilities begin to take shape. The proverbial promised land isn't a myth—it's real, and it's waiting for you. This is your moment. Take it.

KEY TAKEAWAYS

➤ Rebuilding your financial future is an opportunity to create a secure and stable life through consistent small actions, discipline, and thoughtful planning.

➤ Bankruptcy is not an end but a beginning, offering a clean slate to pursue your goals and dreams with renewed confidence and clarity.

➢ Understanding budgeting, credit, and debt management empowers you to make informed decisions and avoid past mistakes.

➢ Setting small, achievable goals and celebrating progress builds momentum and confidence, turning small wins into lasting success.

➢ Life's unpredictability requires preparation—plan ahead, anticipate risks, and embrace the fresh start bankruptcy provides to navigate challenges and achieve financial independence.

Epilogue

"It's never too late to be what you might have been."
— **George Eliot**

Congratulations.

You've just done something most people never do: face the truth about debt with honesty, courage, and curiosity. That alone sets you apart. You chose to understand while others hide, avoid, or silently carry the weight. And that decision? It's the start of your freedom.

Now you see what few people realize:

Bankruptcy is not the end—it's a legal tool, a reset, a path. A quiet, powerful act of self-respect. It's how people just like you choose debt relief with dignity. It's how they reclaim their peace of mind, their power, and their future.

This book didn't just teach you about the process of bankruptcy. It handed you permission to let go of shame. It gave you a way to move from financial survival to emotional and financial stability. This is the magic of bankruptcy—the unseen shift that happens when you decide you deserve better.

But here's the truth you can't ignore:

Knowing this and doing nothing is still a choice. And it's the costliest one. Every day you wait, stay stuck in fear, minimum payments, or denial—you lose time, peace, and options. You carry a burden that doesn't belong to you anymore.

You've read the book. You've seen the light through the cracks. Now it's time to act.

Visit **www.TheLadylikeLawyer.com**—it's your launchpad. You'll be matched with a trusted, compassionate bankruptcy lawyer in your area who offers free consultations. I've built a national network of professionals who share my mission: debt relief with dignity.

And if you're not quite ready to speak with a lawyer—or you live in an area where legal options feel overwhelming—I also offer 1:1 coaching to help you understand your choices, navigate fear, and move forward with clarity and confidence. Coaching is not legal advice but guidance rooted in truth, compassion, and experience.

Here's your next step plan:

1. Go to **www.TheLadylikeLawyer.com** and answer a few quick questions.
2. Get connected with a local attorney for a free consultation, or book a coaching session with me if you're first looking for clarity and emotional support.
3. Start moving forward—with support, strategy, and someone in your corner.

And as you move forward, know this:

You can rebuild. You can reset. You can rest.

You can create a life where debt no longer writes your story—you do.

You can stop surviving and start thriving.

You can live with dignity, move with freedom, and build something new.

Because it's not too late to be what you might have been.

And your comeback?

It starts now.

With belief in your journey,
Adrienne Hines
Bankruptcy Lawyer, Advocate, and Fierce Believer in Fresh Starts

About Adrienne Hines

Adrienne Hines is a seasoned bankruptcy attorney with nearly 30 years
of experience helping individuals and
families achieve debt relief with dignity.
Based in Northwest Ohio, Adrienne
is passionate about dispelling bankruptcy myths through her educational
content, including her popular social
media videos, where she breaks down
complex financial concepts into relat-
able, easy-to-understand advice. Her
compassionate and informative approach ensures clients explore all
their options to regain financial stability. Adrienne's mission is to
empower people to navigate debt challenges with confidence and
clarity, restoring hope and providing a path to a brighter financial
future through debt relief with dignity.

What Adrienne's Clients Are Saying...

"Hi, Adrienne. I just wanted to thank you. You brought such peace to this process for me. We have two special needs boys, and we're drowning in medical debt and debt from trying to survive the economy. You have such a calm about you. Thank you for all you do!"

- Jeremy S.

"I was following you on social media for about a year before I contacted your office. I always thought of bankruptcy in a "Yeah, but I'd never actually do it" way until I saw an article about you living in my hometown! I immediately got excited and hopeful that we could actually go through with it because you, of all lawyers, would be our lawyer! Your content is so incredibly comforting and validating, so never stop doing that."

- Sarah A.

"I had an exceptional experience with Attorney Adrienne Hines. She is very warm and welcoming. She and her paralegal worked around my busy work schedule, and they were detail-oriented and easy to communicate with. They truly have your best interest at heart and will assist in any way possible. I never felt alone; I have zero regrets!"

- Sabrina R.

"Adrienne has been a huge help in my bankruptcy case. She answered my questions promptly, with discretion, and with care. I learned a lot from her TikTok videos and our conversations. Most importantly, she answered me with care and respect. She took the embarrassing feeling out of filing for bankruptcy. I highly recommend her."

\- Randy D.

"I wish bankruptcy would be less of a taboo topic to discuss. Nothing to be asha\med of."

"You have changed my life. Thank you for helping me feel comfortable with my situation and decision to move forward."

"You literally saved my life. I was having such dark thoughts and no way out when I came across your content. You gave me the courage to talk to a lawyer, and I just had my bankruptcy hearing, and I feel the weight of the world lifted off my shoulders!"

"I've been so stressed because of this debt. You have been a Godsend to me."

"I fell for the debt relief trap. All they did was take my money. Filing bankruptcy is slowly changing my life and was the best decision I ever made."

"Negative equity... or paying a car off quickly and responsibly. Bankruptcy gave me clarity to avoid these traps."

"These lenders are like glorified loan sharks! I would have kept paying them if I hadn't learned that bankruptcy was an option."

"I just assumed that there were laws that would not let lenders charge me 499% interest! Imagine my surprise when I realized what I'd gotten myself into."

"I always assumed I couldn't file because I own a home, but now I'm credit card debt-free!"

"I was drowning in loans and credit cards. Filing was my lifeline."

"I wish I had known sooner. This process changed everything for me."

"Thank you for helping me understand the rules. I feel so FREE!"

"I've been taught financial lessons that many people weren't taught and had to learn the hard way."

"I followed the link to the Chapter 7 calculator and just did my consultation. You are amazing!"

*"I filed Chapter 7 today because of you.
I couldn't be more relieved."*

*"Your guidance and enthusiasm made this
process so much less stressful."*

*"Your advice videos helped me take the leap of
filing for bankruptcy, and it's so worth it!"*

*"My credit score jumped 180 points within two weeks after
filing. Such a myth that you're tainted for 7 years!"*

*"Listen to this woman... I'm $50k less in debt,
discharged in December, and thriving!"*

*"Now I'm credit card debt-free, discharged,
and looking at new cars as we type!"*

*"You've given me the confidence and knowledge to
rebuild. Thank you from the bottom of my heart."*

*"I was facing bankruptcy or suicide. The shame was
unbearable. Now I am no longer ashamed."*

www.ingramcontent.com/pod-product-compliance
Lightning Source LLC
Chambersburg PA
CBHW070808280326
41934CB00012B/3111